Readers Praise Kathleen Shelby Boyett's Books:

Praise for *Iwo Jima Changed Everything*

"The *real* story of a man's overseas duty during World War II, and his life in general, both before and after the war. Poignant and bittersweet, Ms. Boyett weaves a touching tale that only a daughter can, finding out in retrospect how those experiences on Iwo Jima shaped her father's heart and influenced her life. A touching testimony to the veterans of that terrible war, *Iwo Jima Changed Everything* is well worth reading."

> Bryan Boyett, author of
> *Unsung Heroes: Voices of WWII*

"Shame on you for writing such an interesting book. I started reading at 8:50 and didn't stop 'til I finished. It's well written, well documented, well everything!"

> Bill Norberg
> World War II Veteran

Praise for *John Markham: The Origins of Virginia's Pirate*

"It is a fascinating read, and I am now convinced that John Markham was the ancestor of Chief Justice John Marshall. Many cheers to Kathleen Shelby Boyett for her great job of research!"

David W. Morgan

"My copy came yesterday. LOVING IT. I am impressed with the research and thought that went into this book. It is I who thank *you* and am grateful you are devoted to telling our ancestors' stories, putting a voice and flesh to our people."

Robin Coffman

"Bought and read your book. I LOVE IT!!!!!!!! Never be afraid to toot your own horn!"

Rhonda Rogers Corbett

Praise for *On Both Sides*

"I marvel at your research. The detail you bring to the reader makes the time come alive."

Robert T. Shelby

Praise for *Uprooted: An American Family Saga, Volume One*

"It is so well written that there are not any boring parts at all, as you might expect in a story of one's ancestors. It was such an easy read I finished it in about 3 days. It is not just about whose ancestors were whose, but lots of information about the wars they fought and how their families survived. I am so looking forward to her next research project."

Mary Esposito

Praise for *Free State of Jones and Parallels*

"I have read your book and really enjoyed it. I find that your book gives a fresh new look at the history and legacy of the Newt Knight clan! The book was well written and easy to read. It is a good addition to anyone's collection of books about Newt Knight and Jones County, Mississippi."

Robert J. McSwain, Jr., author of *Early Perry County, Mississippi Newspapers*

Books by Kathleen Shelby Boyett

Boys in Butternut
Destiny on the North Sea
Fallen Sons
Free State of Jones and Parallels
Free State of Jones: The True Story
Flying Fearlessly
Iwo Jima Changed Everything
John Markham: The Origins of Virginia's Pirate
Keep 'em Flying
Letters from a Wounded Soldier
Letters of a Reluctant Confederate
Life and War
Life and War Book 2
Manifest Destiny
On Both Sides
Patriots, Hessians, Refugees & Spies
Secrets of a Backcountry Cemetery
Secrets of the Williams Cemetery
Uprooted: An American Family Saga, Volume One
Uprooted: An American Family Saga, Volume Two
Uprooted: An American Family Saga, Volume Three
Women of Pioneer Spirit

Edited works: Adventuresome Caribbean Pirates; A Path of Lasting Tranquility; Backcountry Beginnings; Bold Men of the American Frontier; Born in the Waxhaws; Captured in Colonial America, Captured in the Old West; Captured on the Prairie; Courageous Women of the American Frontier; Echoes from The Great War ;The Paiute Princess; Women of the Revolution; and More Women of Revolution.

Life and War Book 2
Veterans of World War II

Kathleen Shelly Boyett

Life and War

Book 2

Veterans of World War II

BY

Kathleen Shelby Boyett

Searching Mink Publishing
Charlotte, North Carolina

On the cover: Jesse Oxendine.

Parts of Ray Tarte's story were written from information provided in the Kevin Callahan interviews. Ralph Easterling's interview was co-conducted by Bryan Boyett. Photographs from private collections are designated by the veteran's initials.

Contents

We shall go on to the end. We shall fight in France, we shall fight on the seas and oceans, we shall fight with growing confidence and growing strength in the air; we shall defend our island, whatever the cost may be. We shall fight on the beaches, we shall fight on the landing grounds, we shall fight in the fields and in the streets, we shall fight in the hills; **we shall never surrender**...

Winston Churchill
Prime Minister of the United Kingdom
4 June 1940

Lieutenant Raymond Leo Tarte, Jr.

Lt. Ray Tarte (RT)
USAAF, 8th Air Force, 301st Fighter Wing,
507th Fighter Group, 465th Squadron

I discovered Ray Tarte's story due to my husband's appearance on a local television show with a World War II veteran. This morning appearance led me to meet one of the news anchors and thus to hear the story of his wife's grandfather during the war. I knew immediately that I wanted to include Ray's story in an upcoming book.

As a youth, Ray Tarte lived in East St. Paul and attended Hastings High School. He remembered that he was at Tanner's Lake fishing when he heard about the attack on Pearl Harbor over the radio.

Tarte's wife, Roselyn, was also from East St. Paul. Ray married Rosie on the day he graduated from flight training and got his wings. His pay jumped immediately from $80 per month to $429 per month, which was quite a jump. Everybody wanted to be a fighter pilot back then, for the bravado and the prestige, and also for the luxury: the men's wives could stay with the pilots while at the training air fields and on the troop transport trains, whereas the poor enlisted men's wives could not.

Ray Tarte entered the Army Air Corps when he was twenty-three years old, and exited at age twenty-seven. Ray became a flight instructor and received a great deal of flight time and training in the States, and not just by chance. Tarte had ruptured both eardrums in pressure chamber training because he had a slight cold and didn't realize it. In the pressure chamber, Ray had to put on an oxygen mask and the pressure was lowered to the equivalent of the pressure at 30,000 feet. He had to write a note, which he assumed he was doing normally. Later, he was shown what he had actually written and it was all "looping and distorted." While the rest of his group went off to Europe, he was still recovering from his ruptured eardrums. Those damaged eardrums were the reason why he became a flight instructor, and why he was sent to the Asiatic-Pacific Theater of war, which was actually his preference over the European Theater.

[2]

Tarte trained at two air fields after he joined the 507th Fighter Group, which was first activated at Peterson Field, Colorado on 12 October 1944 and was equipped with the long range version of the Republic P-47 Thunderbolt, the P-47N. Its original squadrons were the 463d, 464th, and 465th Fighter Squadrons. One week later, on 20 October, the Fighter Group moved to Bruning Army Air Field to begin training, but without yet receiving personnel or other equipment!

Bruning Army Air Field was six miles outside of Bruning, Nebraska, in Thayer County. It was in September of 1942 that twelve land owners received notice from the federal government that they had ten days to move off their farms, including livestock, farm equipment, feed, and all possessions, leaving their crops in the fields. They were compensated approximately $50 an acre. Construction was started immediately on what would become the three runways of the airfield. The first unit arrived for training on 2 August 1943. At its peak of activity, Bruning had 3,077 military and 500 civilian personnel assigned to it. Today, the property is leased to local farmers and a cattle feedlot company. Only one of the three runways is still visible.

Hangar at Bruning Air Field, 2004 (Robert Pearson)

This base provided training for the Consolidated B-24 Liberator heavy bombers and the Republic P-47 Thunderbolt fighter bombers. The 507th Fighter Group, Ray's unit, was there from 20 October through 12 December 1944.

The P-47N was the latest and also the fastest model of Republic's P-47. Nicknamed the "Jug," supposedly because its profile was similar to that of a common milk jug of the time, it was larger and heavier than other planes, and built for long range flying. When fully loaded, the P-47N weighed up to eight tons, making it one of the heaviest fighters of the war. The "Jug" was powered by the powerful Pratt & Whitney R-2800 Double Wasp engine which was also used by the Grumman F6F Hellcat and the Vought F4U Corsair.

Waterloo Milk Company period milk jugs

The P-47N had eight .50 caliber machine guns, which were incredibly powerful, and it had the capability to carry five-inch rockets or a bomb load of 2,500 pounds. A new wing was designed with two fifty-gallon fuel tanks and squared-off wingtips which improved the roll rate. The redesign was successful in extending the plane's range to about 2,000 miles. The belly gas tanks carried 1,200 gallons. When these were empty, the pilot simply pulled a lever and dropped them in the ocean. Should an emergency have occurred, a forced belly landing on a full gas tank would have been a death sentence.

P-47N Fighter-Bombers in formation

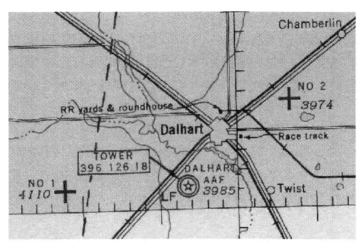

Map of Dalhart, TX, 1945 (Chris Kennedy)

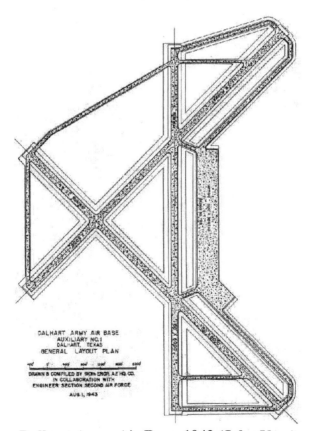

DALHART ARMY AIR BASE
AUXILIARY NO. 1
DALHART, TEXAS
GENERAL LAYOUT PLAN

DRAWN & COMPILED BY 910th ENGR. AE HQ. CO.
IN COLLABORATION WITH
ENGINEER SECTION SECOND AIR FORCE

AUG. 1, 1943

Dalhart Army Air Base, 1943 (John Voss)

[6]

On 15 December 1944, the 507th moved to Dalhart Army Air Field, outside of Dalhart, Texas. There Tarte received training to prepare him for assignment in the Asiatic-Pacific Theater of Operations. For four months he received combat training for long-range escort, strafing, and dive bombing.

Dalhart Air Field opened in May 1942, at the behest of three prominent local men who wanted to do something more for the war effort. In September 1942, cadets began arriving for training at the school.

The 878th, 879th, and 880th Glider Training Squadrons were established at the base. Cadets learned the necessary skills with towed flights on a 350 foot nylon rope behind a C-47 Skytrain aircraft.

CG-4 Glider being towed by a C-47 Skytrain, 1943

Transferred to the Second Air Force, under the jurisdiction of II Bomber Command, by February 1943 the new mission of the base was to be a heavy bomber aircrew replacement training center, flying the B-17 Flying Fortress and the B-24 Liberator. In March 1944, the mission of Dalhart was again changed, as B-29 Superfortress crews were needed in the Pacific Theater for the bombardment of Japan. The 507th

Fighter Group trained P-47N Thunderbolt pilots in very long range escort missions to support XX Bomber Command B-29 Superfortresses on bombing missions to the Japanese Home Islands. During training, the pilots would sit in the cockpit for hours learning where all the controls were. The men had to be able to point to the instruments and dials while blindfolded, with the instructor standing on the wing watching them.

The 463rd, 464th, and 465th Fighter Squadrons, flying the P-47 Thunderbolt, were deployed to the Twentieth Air Force in Okinawa in late April. Ray's squadron, the 465th, was composed of flight instructors like himself. On 24 April, the group departed Dalhart for shipment overseas, staging out of Fort Lawton, Washington.

Ray and his squadron saw various islands while being transported on an escort carrier across the Pacific to Ie Shima. The escort carrier, also called a "jeep carrier" or more affectionately, a "baby flattop," was typically half the length and with a third the displacement of larger fleet carriers. Although these craft were slower, carried fewer planes, and were less well armed and armored, escort carriers were cheaper and could be built quickly – an advantage in war time. Tarte was able to visit the islands of Majuro, Eniwetok, Saipan, Tinian, and Guam.

Ray liked Majuro, in the Marshall Islands, which had a deep harbor that the carrier and other ships could enter, and even considered going back there on a trip after the war. Several of the pilots were taken on a boat to an island twenty-five miles away and met natives who lived basically in isolation from other tribes. The children there had never seen an ice cold soft drink or even an orange, and they loved the chocolate candy bars the pilots gave them. Ray did note that the women wore nothing above the waist. Majura was surrounded by other islands that still contained Japanese military personnel that had been bypassed by the Allies' island hopping. The squadron stood ready to attack them, recognizing that there were still casualties among those locals who were fighting the Japanese. However, the "higher-ups" did not allow the P-47N pilots to have any ammo or to fly missions against the nearby islands. They were saved for duty escorting B-29s.

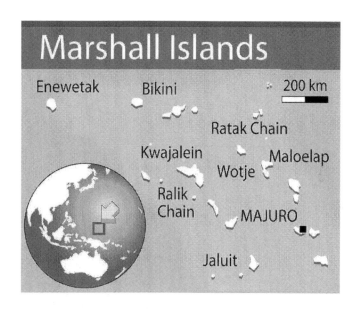

Majuro air strip today

[9]

"Major Hemphill's Expendables" (RT)
(Ray is in lower left of photo)

Tarte trained for two weeks in catapulting a plane off of a carrier, which had never been done before with a heavy P-47N. Ray figured someone of higher rank, not a mere 2nd Lieutenant, would be the first to try catapulting a P-47N off of the carrier for landing on Majuro, but instead he was the one performing the difficult feat. He should have known that: "the lower the rank, the more expendable."

The 507th arrived in the Asiatic-Pacific Theater 24 June, and was stationed at Ie Shima in the Ryukyu Islands, off Okinawa, and was assigned to the 301st Fighter Wing. The rest of the Fighter Group's history is briefly summarized here: on the first of July it began flying airstrikes from Ie Shima, targeting enemy ships, railroad bridges, airfields, factories, and barracks in Japan, Korea, and China. The group encountered little enemy opposition on these strikes. On 8 August the group escorted Boeing B-29 Superfortress bombers on a raid on Yawata, Japan, during which the 507th faced stiff opposition and shot down several Japanese fighters. The 507th earned a Distinguished Unit Citation when it engaged and destroyed Japanese interceptor aircraft during a long-range fighter sweep to Korea on 13 August. After the Japanese surrender, the 507th moved to Yontan Airfield, Okinawa on 19 January of 1946, and was inactivated there on 27 May 1946.

When the 465th arrived at its station in the Asiatic-Pacific Theater, Ie Shima – only four miles off the coast of Okinawa and the closest airfield to Japan – the island had three runways and three squadrons of fighters. The island was two miles wide and eight miles long and unfortunately, it was bombed by the Japanese every night. Tarte remembered that he didn't want to dive into the air raid ditches because of the centipedes that lived in then, and he often stayed in his bunk during the raids. On Ie Shima the pilots stayed in four-man tents with a wooden floor and four beds in the corner, plus room for a card table. One of Tarte's tent mates was a flight officer.

Pilots were issued air mattresses, which ground crew did not get. Ray arranged for his crew chief to get an air mattress but on the first night he tried to use it, during the nightly air raid the spent anti-aircraft ammunition put a hole in it – so much for comfort. Tarte didn't even go into the trench that night, but did put on his helmet. The pilots were less affected by the Japanese night attacks than the ground crews were. The pilots had become accustomed to the danger of flying. The night attacks, normally consisting of two Jap planes, dropping two bombs, was the ground crews' only exposure to lethal combat risk. Once, Ray and some other pilots lit up cigarettes during one air raid – a large "no-no" as it could cause the enemy plane to spot a man's position – and the ground crew in the trench threatened to shoot the pilots if they didn't put the cigarettes out, and Ray believed they meant it.

One time, when Ray went for a walk on Ie Shima with three other pilots, all carrying their .45s, a ragged, shirtless Japanese soldier surrendered to them. This was a very rare occurrence, as most Japs would rather starve than surrender, due to their military training. The man just came out of the brush with his arms raised. He had no rifle and Tarte and the other men didn't think to search him. The Base Intelligence Officer must have given them heck for that slip-up when they turned the man over upon arrival back at base camp.

Because Ie Shima was only four miles from Okinawa, Ray was able to watch the kamikazes going in to attack the U.S. ships. The antiaircraft fire from the Navy ships was impressive.

At Ie Shima, each of the three squadrons had their own landing strip and each had fifty pilots and twenty-five planes. The pilots did not fly two days in a row so as to avoid fatigue. Kyushu – the third biggest island of Japan and the most southwesterly of its four main islands – was about 350 miles away and thus a typical mission might last six hours. On most missions, all twenty-five planes of a squadron took off, and sometimes more, as another squadron joined them. This large mass of planes seemed to be enough to intimidate the Japanese and keep them from taking to the skies in retaliation. Normally,

Major Hemphill, the Executive Officer of the 465th, was in charge of the missions but sometimes Major Rice, the squadron commander, led the squadron. As a Lieutenant, Tarte followed rather than led the missions.

Ray thought these squadrons were the only fighters in the Pacific with *color* gun camera footage. The problem was that there was no facility to develop color film on base, so it had to be flown to Hawaii, developed, and then flown back. This caused considerable delay before they could view their films. The cameras could be switched on without firing the guns.

Ray felt that the "best missions" were when four planes could go to Japan and seek "targets of opportunity" in Japan such as boats, bridges, or cities. Naturally this was more of a "stealth" mission than was escorting the lumbering B-29's. If it was a short mission, the P-47N could carry 2,500 pound bombs under the wings and one 1,000 pound bomb under the belly. For long-range missions the planes were forced to carry extra gas tanks instead of bombs, which made the plane much heavier and also made it harder for the pilot to achieve take-off and landing.

One of the most boring missions was to fly air cover for Ie Shima, which involved four planes circling like buzzards over the island for five hours. As small as the island was, it was a wonder all the pilots were not dizzy from circling. All pilots had to take their turn at this necessary job. After dark, night fighters took over that task.

Each pilot had a survival kit with a raft, canteen, waterproof silk maps, and each carried a .45 pistol. Ray remembered that no one ever ditched a P-47 in the ocean because no one had ever heard of anyone surviving that. The front scoop on the plane would make the impact like hitting a brick wall. If a pilot was forced to leave his plane, he would bail out, but even that was not without danger – the pilot could strike the tail of the plane upon exit. Even turning the plane upside down and falling out didn't stop the risk completely, as the pilot could just hit a different part of the tail.

Ray Tarte with his P-47N (RT)

Tarte spent most of his missions dropping many bombs on bridges and shooting other targets with his .50 caliber guns, which could do quite a lot of damage. Radar stations were an important target. Over Japan, he never saw any Japanese fighters, probably because the Japanese knew they were coming with notice from those radar stations. Ray flew some missions with Navy and Marine fighters and they found that the P-47N was faster than the Corsair. The Navy fighters would fly from a carrier and meet the USAAF planes over the target. The Marines would fly their Corsairs to the Ie Shima airfield and fly with Ray's group up to Japan. They all participated in trying to hit a radar station situated on a long rocky promontory sticking out into the sea, on the south part of Kyushu, but with no success.

Ray flew in the longest fighter mission of World War II – an eight hour and twenty-seven minute mission from the fighter group's base at Ie Shima to near Seoul, Korea – which completely surprised the Japanese; they never dreamed that the P-47N could travel that far. Tarte's unit destroyed twenty-three Japanese aircraft. One pilot shot down five aircraft on that one mission, making him an ace. The pilots carried two canteens of water and no food. They could regulate their temperature by the height they flew: below 10,000 feet it got hot, but above 10,000 feet, the temperature was comfortable. It was not comfortable on one's backside, however, to sit on one's parachute for that long. This flight earned Tarte's unit a Presidential Unit Citation.

Tarte had started out in the Pacific with a brand new, shiny, P-47N, and six months later, it was all "beat up" – shot full of holes from ground fire, the openings of which had been patched-up. Ray felt that the wear on the plane would eventually have worn it out or made it unsafe and he did not think he would have survived the war if the U.S. had invaded mainland Japan.

One of Ray's last missions would be an important one and one he would never forget. On 9 August 1945, Ray flew with the fighter escort for the Nagasaki atomic bomb mission. He personally saw the Nagasaki mushroom cloud come up through the regular clouds after the bomb exploded, from what he believed was about twenty-five or thirty miles away. It was a cloudy day and the bomb's cloud looked like every other white cloud except that it was rising quickly. He did not feel any concussion from the blast at the distance he was away from ground zero.

The first atomic bomb, which fell on Hiroshima, was a complete surprise to the men, but this time they had been briefed on the bomb and knew what their mission was sent to do before they left Ie Shima for Japan. The idea of having P-47Ns close by the B-29s when the bomb went off was that their presence would prevent the Japanese Zeroes from taking off in pursuit. The Zero fighters avoided the U.S. fighters, but they would come up after the slower B-29s.

Atomic bomb "Fat Man" mushroom cloud over Nagasaki, Japan (taken from a B-29)

At the time, the mission did not seem very exciting. Tarte and the other pilots flew over land at about 10,000 feet above the clouds and could not go over the target area. Since the fighters were above the clouds, the pilots never saw the B-29s – with Bockscar, the B-29 that dropped the bomb, flying at 28,900 feet – at any time during the mission.

B-29 "Bockscar" nose art

After the bomb went off, all the fighter planes turned and took gun camera footage of the mushroom cloud and then turned for home. The fighters tried to keep radio silence, which was important. Ray never heard the B-29s on the radio. The squadron commander may have had radio contact with them, but Ray never heard anything. To escort "nothing" to Japan, as Ray describes, must have been a strange feeling.

The following day after the bombing, Ray flew to Nagasaki with three other P-47 pilots and flew over the devastated city at about 1,500 feet. No one at that time knew about the dangers of radiation. The men flew through different colored dust clouds, pink and white and brown, a frightening, dangerous thought to us now. Still alive into his nineties, Ray felt it hadn't hurt him in the long run.

Visibility that day was pretty good, and the men could see that the city was "gone." Almost everything below them was flattened. Tarte was able to see what an atomic bomb really did. He was familiar with Nagasaki before this because the Japanese fleet, bottled up like cordwood in the Nagasaki harbor by the U.S. Navy, was used as a target by the pilots if they had to get rid of their unused bombs at the end of a cancelled mission.

Tarte told the story in his own words:

> We were scheduled to escort the B-29s and we knew at the time that we were escorting the B-29 that had the atomic bomb on it, so we all flew up there . . . We had to stay back aways from Nagasaki at the time, where they had finally decided that they were going to drop the bomb. We were close and we were above the clouds. It was clouds all over the place. So we're tooling around out there, waiting for the B-29 that went in with the atomic bomb to come out so we can escort them back home, and all of a sudden one of our pilots shouted, "There she goes!" Well, we can't see the ground, we can't see anything but clouds, but all of a sudden, out of the clouds comes this big mushroom cloud, so we knew the atomic bomb went off. Well, you know, it wasn't spectacular. You know it would have been spectacular if the weather was clear and we could have seen this thing go off, but it didn't turn out that way. Anyway, it was an historic moment, and we all knew it up there. So we all turned our planes around and aimed it at the big cloud

that was going up in the air and pulled our trigger that just triggered the gun camera and we had color film in our gun cameras, so we all got a picture of the atomic mushroom cloud. So then we escorted them back home to Okinawa and the mission was over. So it should have been an exciting mission, but it was kind of a letdown. It was just another mission.

So, the next day we took a flight of planes and we flew up to Nagasaki. Now we had been over Nagasaki quite a few times. Any time we had a bombing mission and we couldn't get rid of our bombs because of the weather or something, we flew over Nagasaki and dropped the bombs on the navy ships in the harbor just to get rid of them because we couldn't go back home with them on. So we knew Nagasaki. It was a big city but it had a range of low hills going right through the middle of it. Okay, now that made a difference when that atomic bomb went off because this range of hills protected, not completely, but some part of the city. So the next day a flight of us went up to Nagasaki and we knew the war was going to be over momentarily and we didn't worry about any Jap planes or getting shot at. We flew over Nagasaki and we were stunned by the destruction down there. Everything was leveled. The sky around us, the air around us, was all different colors: pink, brown, you name it. The colors were there and it was kind of pretty. And we were so dumb, we didn't know that that was dust from this atomic bomb that could have been really, really radioactive. They didn't tell us any of that. We didn't know that. So we're tooling around there 1,500 feet over Nagasaki. We thought that was a blast. The dust from the day before was still in the air, and of course with the sun shining and everything, it made all these different colors.

[19]

I could see no activity on the ground whatsoever. In fact you could only see maybe a half a brick building standing, or a wall, or something like that. Otherwise it was completely gone.

The first one on Hiroshima – nobody knew about that. The only ones that knew about it were the ones that were involved and there was no fighter escort, no nothing for the B-29s that went up there. They dropped the bomb and got out. But the one at Kokura, supposedly Kokura, and Nagasaki, we were briefed. We knew that we were escorting the B-29 that had the atomic bomb on it. So it was kind of exciting, you know.

. . . We didn't run into any Jap planes because they were afraid of us. They knew that if they came up, we'd shoot them down because we had so much firepower. So they never came up when the fighters were around.

Perhaps Ray never expected that people would be anxious to hear about his escort flight to Nagasaki, but his participation in the event earned him at least a small measure of fame.

Tarte did not ever get airsick during the war, but he came close once when in a C-47 on his way to Tokyo four days after the war's end. He felt that being enclosed in the body of the plane instead of being in the cockpit was probably what caused it. He and three other pilots "bummed a ride" up to Tokyo and Ray called it the scariest thing he did in the whole war. When the pilots were on the trains the Japanese were "looking daggers" at them. The four of them only had .45 pistols on their hips. The pilots ate fish at a half-collapsed building occupied by the Americans just off the Emperor's Palace and it was the first time Tarte had a meal off of "regular plates" in many months. In the moat of the palace were large carp and this was presumably from where their lunch came. While in Japan, Ray noted that there could be more people waiting on the train platform than there was space on the train, but the military men were always let on first. The Japanese he saw were mostly women and they had malnutrition sores. The cigarettes the pilots gave them were treated like gold. A rotten smell pervaded the town and a lot of windows were blown out from the bombing. The war had definitely been hard on the Japanese people.

After the war Ray went into air traffic control as a career, which he really enjoyed. He became an instructor in Farmington, Minnesota, and retired from work in 1974. Ray enjoyed fishing for walleye and became an avid fisherman in retirement. He kept good records of how many fish he caught, and one year he recorded 764 walleyes caught. He and his wife, Rosie, attended every one of his squadron reunions that they possibly could.

Ray lived to be ninety-four years old and enjoyed seventy-two years of happy marriage with Rosie.

Yeoman Willard "Bill" Norberg

Bill Norberg, U.S. Navy, 1945 (WN)

[23]

It was thirty degrees below zero in Lemington, Wisconsin the day Bill Norberg was born. It was the 13th of November, 1922, and his parents were Gustaf and Ruth Swanson Norberg. Gustaf immigrated to America from Sweden.

Sadly, Bill's mother became ill when he was only four years old, and this deprived him of memories of a mother's hugs. He does remember gathering around the family's crystal radio set and neighbors taking turns listening to "squeaks and scratches and occasional music or words" from a radio station in Chicago. One childhood memory is of a faithful dog:

> We had a dog named "Buster." He was a beautiful, obedient collie dog who looked out for the whole family and our cattle, too. One day I wandered into the pasture and the bull decided he didn't want any interlopers around so he started after me. Good old Buster came to the rescue, grabbing the bull by the nostrils and shaking him violently until I could climb through the barbed wire fence. I left some skin from my right eyebrow on that barbed wire and still have the scar to prove it!

By 1928, Bill's mother was so ill that she needed special care, and the family abandoned their farm and moved to Chicago. Bill and his brother went to live with good family friends, the Andersons, a kind and generous couple who had offered to keep the boys while Bill's father found a suitable home. When he did find a place, it was directly across the back alley from the Andersons, so Bill's life was not totally disrupted a second time. Later, during the Great Depression, Bill and his brother spent some time in a children's home about two hours west of Chicago. This was a sad time for him, and one he has mostly tried to forget.

While there, Bill remembers that in 1932 or 1933, Admiral Richard Byrd came and spoke at the high school about his Antarctic adventures. "Now that was exciting! It piqued my interest in the Navy and had some influence in my choice of service branches several years later."

Then, in 1934, Bill's father was able to make arrangements for Bill and his brother to leave the children's home and join him in Massachusetts, where Bill stayed throughout his high school years.

In the fall of 1940, Bill went to work at Bell Woolen Mills in Worcester, earning forty cents an hour. He had a room at a small hotel for $2 a week, and ate at a boarding house where he was given two meals plus a packed lunch for $5 a week, leaving him with a balance of $9 to spend as he wished.

Although there are parts of his childhood best forgotten, Bill is pleased, however, to remember his days in the U.S. Navy. He sailed on the USS *Enterprise* for four years, and saw the entire Pacific War from a command position, as the Captain's Yeoman.

Bill enlisted on 14 February 1941 in Springfield, Massachusetts. He was then sent to Newport, Rhode Island, on Narragansett Bay. There, the winds howled and the barracks were drafty.

For two weeks, his company was assigned to the USS *Constellation*, which was an old wooden sailing ship that had been launched on 26 August 1854 and is now preserved as a museum ship in Baltimore, Maryland. She was the last sail-only warship designed and built by the United States Navy. During the Civil War, the *Constellation* was dispatched to the Mediterranean Sea to protect American commerce, as its lack of a steam engine made it unsuitable for blockading the Southern coast. For the first six months of 1942, the Commander-in-Chief of the Atlantic Fleet, Admiral Royal E. Ingersoll, commanded from the ship's eighty-eight-year-old decks. Being taller than previous generations of sailors, the World War II sailors often bumped their heads on the overhead.

Norberg in 1941 (WN)

[26]

USS Constellation, 1854 as a museum ship

Bill added that:

We slept in hammocks (now that's a trick to get into the "sack" and maintain one's balance to stay in there. Slackers would get a solid whomp on their bottoms if they stayed in their hammocks too long after 5:30 morning reveille. I didn't appreciate such and managed to get up just about reveille so that I could finish all my clean-up duties in the "head" before the stampede started.

Norberg's class graduated in mid-April and was given a week's leave. Unfortunately, while Bill was at home, he contacted pleurisy and had to wire his base to ask for an extension of leave until he recovered. No such luck for Bill – the return wire instructed him to "Return to base immediately, medical attention awaits you." When he got back to his barracks, though, no doctor ever called to see him.

Bill was then loaded onto a troop train and shipped off to San Diego for communications school. The train stopped for eight hours in Buffalo, and his bunk mate invited him to visit his home there, a nice diversion. Four days later, Bill arrived in San Diego and his sister and aunt were there to meet him at the station. This was the start of a more pleasant time period for Bill. He was able to enjoy many weekends at his aunt and uncle's home, and visited such sites as Mission Beach, La Jolla, the famous zoo, and a small country church in Dulzura. Friends who lived near the little church owned an orange grove, and Bill ate oranges "fresh off the trees" to his heart's content.

Norberg taught himself shorthand during communications school, as his ambition was to become a Chief Yeoman and shorthand was a requirement for that position.

A sailor friend and Bill bought a steam iron for $2.50 and earned "beaucoup bucks" pressing uniforms for sailors in the barracks at a cost of 75¢ for blues and 50¢ for whites. Norberg's sister was unable to work, as she was recovering from tuberculosis, so Bill used to give her a little money to help her along. He felt she deserved more than he was able to give for being a loving sister to him.

Norberg was assigned what would be considered by most to be a less-than-choice duty, yet he didn't mind:

> Each Saturday we were to be on the parade ground for Captain's inspection. About the second or third week I swooned a bit while waiting on the tarmac in the hot sun and was sent back to barracks and told not to go to inspection anymore. I was assigned to cleaning the heads, instead. That was a snap and I was always

ready in my dress whites to hit the front gate for liberty about the time inspection was over.

Another duty assigned to Bill was more interesting. He and two other sailors were given the kitchen assignment of cleaning the pie plates that contained unfinished pies – chocolate, apple, and cherry, as he recalls. "Why we didn't balloon in the mid-section is a mystery but we really engorged on those pies," Bill chuckled.

Wavy-haired "man of the waves" (WN)

His first training course was fourteen weeks long and Norberg experienced a heated competition for top grade with a big Texan, whom Norberg referred to as "Lucky." In week thirteen, Bill was two points behind Lucky. "Then, the medical staff pulled a surprise inspection and Lucky was found to have gonorrhea and he was moved back "three weeks or until healed" and I was able to walk across the platform to receive congratulations from the base commander."

Bill was chosen in the draft for the USS *Enterprise*, which called for fourteen billets, one of which was for a yeoman striker in the Captain's office. "That plum turned out to be mine!" Bill rejoiced.

USS *Wharton*, San Francisco Bay, 1941

He sailed to Pearl Harbor on the troop transport, the USS *Wharton*, a converted luxury liner. Originally named the *Southern Cross*, the ship sailed for the Munson Steamship Line in its South American service. Munson operated the ship on the New York to Rio de Janeiro, Montevideo, and Buenos Aires route. *Southern Cross* was acquired by the Navy on 8 November 1939, renamed *Wharton,* and designated a transport with the hull number AP-7. The *Wharton* departed Brooklyn on 7 January 1941, bound for Guantanamo Bay, Cuba, where she conducted shakedown before proceeding through the Panama Canal to her new home port, Mare Island, California. Assigned to the Naval Transportation Service, the *Wharton* transported service personnel and their families, as well as cargo, between San Francisco, San Diego, and Pearl Harbor. On 17 April 1944, while entering Seeadler Harbor at Manus, in northern Papua New Guinea, she ran aground due to an inaccurate chart and poor placement of buoys marking the channel. After the ship had been refloated on the 18th, a quick check revealed no damage to her hull or machinery. The *Wharton* supported the invasions of the Philippines and of Okinawa and was awarded three battle stars for her World War II service.

Bill's trip aboard the USS *Wharton* took seven days and could have been an enjoyable time, but Bill was assigned painting duty. He was a couple of decks below topside, and on the first day, as he was on a ladder, with paint brush and bucket, the division lieutenant came in with his starched white uniform and stood directly below Bill's ladder. Bill had what he called "a woozy spell" and the paint bucket fell from the ladder to the deck, "but only after splattering that battleship gray paint on the lieutenant from chest to feet." Bill was sent topside.

The USS *Enterprise* was at sea when Bill arrived in Pearl Harbor, so he spent "a delightful week at the Naval Air Station on Ford Island. Guess what we got to do? Paint!"

Then, it came to time to finally board the Big "E." Bill felt overwhelmed at the immensity of the ship at first, as a sailor led him to his new station where he would spend the next four years.

From September to the end of November of 1941, the U.S. was still at peace, and so the Enterprise's cruises were "relaxing." After Bill had gained his sea legs, he enjoyed watching gunnery practice and the take-offs and landings of the pilots from the flight deck, which he found exhilarating. Lord Louis Mountbatten of the British Royal Navy came on the

Enterprise to inspect American carrier operations and the efficiencies the crew had perfected and his subsequent remarks indicated he was greatly impressed with the gunnery, the aircraft operations, and the morale of the ship.

A jaunty Norberg "sees the world" with the Navy (WN)

Then came November 28, 1941. We'd been sent out to sea with orders to deliver a squadron of Marine fighter planes to reinforce the small garrison on Wake Island. Those orders also stipulated that if the Japanese posed any threat whatsoever to let the guns fire away and to let the planes arm and drop their bombs and torpedoes where need be. Before we got back to Pearl Harbor, the Japanese were at war with the United States.

We were due to arrive in Pearl Harbor at 6 pm Saturday evening, December 6th and a yeoman on Admiral Halsey's staff was due to be married in Honolulu at 8 pm that evening. A horrific storm hit our task force two days out of Pearl and we were buffeted about, more so the smaller destroyers accompanying us. They were so tossed about their hulls were creaking and threatened by the possibility of breaking apart, so the task force slowed to a crawl. Fighting the storm had caused the destroyers to expend an undue amount of diesel fuel so when we reached calmer seas we hooked our fueling lines to the small ships and gave them a long drink of diesel. This delayed us to the point that we couldn't make harbor before dark; a new arrival time was set: 11am, Sunday, December 7, 1941. Of course, that yeoman was really upset and as events came about we were able to say his bride to be was likely the first and only bride to be jilted on consecutive days, once for a mini-monsoon and then for the outbreak of a world war.

We went to general quarters early on Sunday 7th, as was customary, due to tensions with Japan and our planes had begun their flight into Ford Island when we heard one pilot shout: "Don't shoot, don't shoot; this is a friendly aircraft." Shortly thereafter we received the radio message: "This is no drill; Pearl Harbor is under

[33]

attack." World War II was underway with Japan's sneak attack on our battleship fleet. The enemy had been intent on sinking our carrier fleet but the *Enterprise*, the *Lexington*, and *Saratoga*, were all at sea. Had any of the three been sunk, the human loss incurred would have been double that of the *Arizona*.

We stayed at battle stations all day December 7th. About 10 am that day our Executive Officer was scanning the horizon and he suddenly made the announcement: "Look out there, boys, that's what's left of our fleet!" Joining ranks with us were three cruisers and several destroyers; it was not a very reassuring moment.

The following evening we entered port to replenish supplies and what would normally take seventeen hours in daylight hours was accomplished in just seven night-time hours as all hands were required to pitch in.

The *Enterprise* hunted for the enemy during December and all through January 1942, but to no avail. On January 18th, she suffered her first wartime shipboard casualty. At about the same time, a Douglas TBD Devastator that carried three airmen was lost. These men survived thirty-four sun-searing days in a canvas raft with little more than a few drops of water and an occasional fish they managed to catch, drifting over 1,000 miles before being rescued.

On February 1st we, along with the *Yorktown*'s task force, hammered the Marshall and Gilbert Islands. To my knowledge, this was the very first offensive action of any American force during World War II and we on *Enterprise* led the way. The attacks were very successful and as we cruised up the Pearl Harbor channel on February 5th we were greeted by hundreds of soldiers, sailors, nurses, Army Air Corps personnel – you name it. We'd struck the first nail in the Japs' coffin and it was time for a celebration. Sailors lined ships and saluted us with shouts of "Hip, hip, hooray; hip, hip, hooray" and we responded in kind. What a morale builder it was!

On 18 April 1942 the *Enterprise* escorted the USS *Hornet* to a spot several hundred miles from Tokyo from where Jimmy Doolittle and his sixteen B-25 bombers took off to "lay a few eggs on Tokyo and give Hirohito something to think about." The *Enterprise*'s part in this operation was to provide fighter protection should the Japanese launch a surprise attack.

The Guadalcanal Campaign stands out in Bill's mind. It began on 7 August 1942, and the *Enterprise* provided support for the Marine landings.

USS *Enterprise* before the war, April 1939

VT-6 TBDs on *Enterprise*, for the Battle of Midway, June 1944

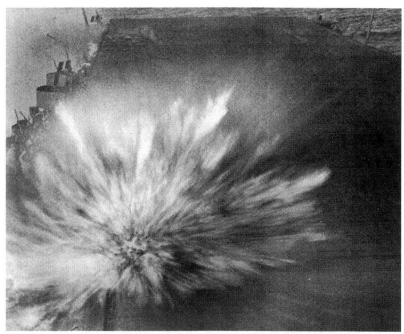

Japanese bomb hits flight deck during the Battle of the Eastern Solomons, August 1942

**Near miss by Jap bomb during the Battle of the
Santa Cruz Islands, 26 October 1942**

The Fifth Fleet at Majuro Atoll 1944
(*Enterprise* on right)

Kamikeze hit on *Enterprise*, 21 May 1945

Then on August 24th we got our initiation to war, being on the receiving end of a couple of heavy bomber attacks. It was impossible to create a foxhole in the steel decks so we stuck to our posts in order not to let our shipmates down even though I and everyone I've talked to, was quite nervous (call it scared if you wish) about the proceedings of that particular day. Out of it, though came a feeling we could "take it" as well as dish it out and that we had a decent chance of survival to live and fight another day and could escape the fate of the carriers *Lexington* and *Yorktown*. We took three good bomb hits that killed several dozen shipmates. Among them was Paul Miller, Storekeeper 2nd class, with whom I was playing checkers when the call to battle stations was sounded at 11 am. We agreed to finish the game when "all clear" was sounded. Paul never lived to see the next day; his entire damage control crew was wiped out by the initial bomb blast. Paul, who'd served a tour of duty in China, told me of his premonition that he wouldn't survive. The blast that killed Paul and his mates also knocked out our steering gear and we drifted helplessly in circles for what seemed like hours with the ship listing to port some 20 degrees. A couple of heroes from the engineering department braved the extreme heat in the engine room and got us on track again – about the time a flight of 30 enemy planes was reported heading toward us. We managed to duck into a rain squall and somehow escaped those enemy bombers.

Norberg experienced some more humorous moments on the *Enterprise* as well as the tragic ones:

Howard Rousseau and I raised the flag upside down in October 1941 and were severely scolded as that's an SOS for a ship in distress. I believe we made a whole lot of sailors happy that day, however, as the Marines were assigned flag-raising duties shortly thereafter.

~~~

Matt Shoemake and I went on shore leave in Honolulu but missed curfew as the last boat to the ship left us behind. We were not supposed to be in the city after dark and had to sneak from bush to bush to evade the many Shore Patrols that wandered the streets. We finally found safe haven at a local hotel where we spent the night. Somehow we managed to board ship the following morning without incident.

Matt Shoemake (WN)

~~~

In April 1942, while participating in the Jimmy Doolittle raid, I was involved in two unusual incidents. We were operating in the North Pacific where rain and mist and cold were the norm.

After delivering a message from the Captain to Admiral Halsey's orderly, I descended the ladder and instead of landing on the hard, steel deck of the catwalk, I lit on something soft – it was the shoe of a very irate admiral who shouted at me: "Damn you!" I answered "Yes, Sir" and took off like a shot, knowing he couldn't possibly recognize me – or catch me. That was my four-word brush with fame as it involved William "Bull" Halsey."

One cold, drizzly night, while on the midnight to 4 am watch, I walked out on the port walkway from the bridge and leaned my head against the steel bulkhead and snoozed a bit. I was awakened by an unearthly noise – somehow, I'd tripped the General Quarters alarm, calling all hands to battle stations. I somehow climbed through the Air Officer's porthole and took off my pea coat as I'd heard someone say: "I don't know, but he was wearing a pea coat." I casually worked my way back past the navigator's desk to my post on the bridge and shivered my way through the rest of the watch. I never revealed my involvement in that escapade for years, fearing the worst.

~~~

Several of us were in the mess hall at lunch hour when a guy at the end of the table crammed the last of a piece of bread into his mouth and showed us the next piece, proclaiming: "Look, guys, I've got raisin bread!" All of us checked ours and found nothing. Shortly a cook came by and we asked him if raisin bread was being served. He laughingly told us: "No, but we've had mice in the bake shop!" Mr. End-of-table wasn't feeling too good at that time!

~~~

Bill returned to the mainland U.S, in July 1943, as the *Enterprise* needed an overhaul. He was given thirty days' leave, and went home to Massachusetts for a restful time. He was surprised to receive some local attention:

My Dad and stepmother and I were invited to attend a community get-together at the Farmers' Hall. So we walked in, and folks were collecting contributions so I put in a pocketful of coins. As the evening progressed,

[41]

the Master of Ceremonies called me on stage to say a few words about life in the Pacific. I was aghast but managed to mumble something or another as it dawned on me – they were recognizing me as guest of honor, being the first of the town's veterans to come back after experiencing combat duty. At the end of the event I was handed a small container – it held over $300 of the townspeople's hard-earned money! I went back to the ship with a deeper appreciation for the folks back home.

As Norberg's battle station throughout the war was on the Captain's bridge, he saw what went on better than most sailors did. He watched Jimmy Doolittle's B-25 bombers take off from the *Hornet* on their way to Tokyo in 1942. He saw innumerable accidents as shot-up planes tried to make one-wheel landings. He says that he was "enrapt as one bomb was dropped from an enemy plane in August 1942 and it grew and grew until finally, I ducked behind the heavy armor plating of the bridge as the bomb exploded a hundred or so feet behind me."

On 14 May 1945, Bill saw a kamikaze as he "whizzed past the starboard wing of the bridge to crash land on the #1 airplane elevator, allowing its 500 lb. bomb to go down three decks and then explode, causing the 13-ton elevator to blow 400 feet in the air before pancaking in the water and floating long enough for several men who'd been blown overboard to climb aboard and await rescue." How incredible this view must have been! This hit knocked the *Enterprise* out of the war and she was retired to Bremerton, Washington, where she was dry-docked and undergoing repairs when the war ended.

The ship was awarded the Presidential Unit Citation, the Navy Unit Citation and the British Royalty Pennant – the only time in its 300-year history that any ship aside from the British Navy had been given that signal honor.

Bill left the *Enterprise* on the ninth of August 1945, just as the second atom bomb was dropped on Nagasaki. He was assigned first to Great Lakes Naval Training Center, Illinois; then to the NATTC Separation Center in Memphis; then to Naval Station, Orange, Texas; then to the Naval brig in New Orleans; and lastly to Naval Center, Norfolk, Virginia. Bill then prepared his own separation papers in December, with a 60-day terminal leave, followed by an honorable discharge effective 10 February 1947.

Stern plate of the USS *Enterprise* CV-6 - The most decorated ship in World War II - River Vale, New Jersey

Navy duty during World War II has proven to be the most exciting time of my life by far and assignment to the USS *Enterprise* was a true blessing in that the ship was in the thick of things from start to finish and the crew was able to come away with the feeling that we had truly contributed to the war effort.

Bill's return to civilian life went fairly smoothly. He returned to Hubbardston, Massachusetts and operated a small poultry farm for a year while working part-time in a nearby stove factory. "My job was to secure the left hand doors to gas and electric heaters as they moved down the assembly line. It was so boring that I transferred to the company's receiving department as soon as possible where the action was a bit heavier."

In 1948, Norberg visited Asheville, North Carolina to see his sister for a short visit:

It was three years later before I got back to my folks in Massachusetts, during which time I'd found a beautiful young lady in Asheville, NC, where both of us worked in the General Accounting Office. Opal Hardister became my wife on May 4, 1950.

In 1950, Bill transferred to the Internal Revenue Service in Greensboro, North Carolina and shortly thereafter Opal was hired by the same agency. She stayed in government service while Bill went to Guilford College for a BA in Business and Accounting and simultaneously worked part-time with a trucking company. He stayed in the trucking business for fourteen years. "All three operations went bankrupt – not due to me, I promise."

In 1969 Bill became Claims Manager for the Belk Stores Group based in Charlotte and retired from there in 1984. Following retirement, he and Opal opened a tax preparation office in Cornelius, North Carolina, which they operated for several years.

Bill humbly speaks with radio and television reporters who are anxious to hear his story. (WN)

Norberg speaking at River Vale, NJ (WN)

Bill Norberg - 2015 with Bill Norberg - 1945
at the Commemoration of the Battle of Midway (WN)

Bill is still active in remembrances of World War II and attends reunions and other functions in various states. I have had an opportunity to know Bill for a few years now, and I feel so fortunate to call him a good friend. He is a quiet, unassuming sort of person, and one would never guess that he had experienced so much in his life and also had played an important part in winning the war in the Asiatic-Pacific Theater – that is, if it were not for that hardly-noticeable USS *Enterprise* cap that he sometimes wears.

Tech Sergeant John Studdard Corzine

Army Air Corps Tech Sgt. John S. Corzine (JC)

[49]

John Corzine, the son of Martin Luther and Mabel Corzine, was born on the fourteenth of February in 1921 in Amity, Arkansas, and lived his younger life in Texarkana, Texas.

John named his school paper in 1932 (JC)

John played the saxophone and the clarinet in his high school band. His after-school hours were spent helping in his father's grocery store.

A very young-looking John Corzine (JC)

When Corzine graduated in 1939, he entered the Army in the Seventh Cavalry Band, which was based at Fort Bliss, Texas. The 7th was the only U.S. cavalry regiment of the period to have a band as the infantry regiments did. This is the same regiment that met defeat at the Little Big Horn under General George

[51]

Armstrong Custer, although it has had a meritorious career otherwise. Forty-five of its soldiers earned the Medal of Honor during the Indian Wars, in addition to nine Presidential Unit Citations, six Valorous Unit Awards, and four Meritorious Unit Commendations.

John followed in his father's footsteps when he entered the Army. Martin Luther Corzine had served in World War I as a Mess Sergeant in France. Pictured at right is his "dog tag" from the war.

Martin (left) and two friends riding an early Harley Davidson motorcycle on the day they volunteered to serve in "The Great War" (JC)

Martin Luther Corzine (JC)

Martin, as did the other men under General John J. Pershing's command, received a letter from him at the end of World War I. The document is a very thoughtful communication to the troops:

MY FELLOW SOLDIERS:

Now that our service with the American Expeditionary Forces is about to terminate, I can not let you go without a personal word. At the call to arms, the patriotic young manhood of America eagerly responded and became the formidable army whose decisive victories testify to its efficiency and its valor. With the support of the nation firmly united to defend the cause of liberty, our army has executed the will of the people with resolute purpose. Our democracy has been tested, and the forces of autocracy have been defeated. To the glory of the citizen-soldier, our troops have faithfully fulfilled their trust, and in a succession of brilliant offensives have overcome the menace to our civilization.

As an individual, your part in the world war has been an important one in the sum total of our achievements. Whether keeping lonely vigil in the trenches, or gallantly storming the enemy's threshold; whether enduring monotonous drudgery at the rear, or sustaining the fighting line at the front, each has bravely and efficiently played his part. By willing sacrifice of personal rights; by cheerful endurance of hardship and privation; by vigor, strength, and indomitable will, made effective by thorough organization and cordial co-operation, you inspired the war-worn Allies with new life and turned the tide of threatened defeat into overwhelming victory.

With a consecrated devotion to duty and a will to conquer, you have loyally served your country. By your exemplary conduct a standard has been established and maintained never before attained by any army. With mind and body as clean and strong as the decisive blows you delivered against the foe, you are soon to return to the pursuits of peace. In leaving the scenes of your victories, may I ask that you carry home your high ideals and continue to live as you have served – an honor to the principles for which you have fought and to the fallen comrades you leave behind.

It is with pride in our success that I extend to you my sincere thanks for your splendid service to the army and to the nation.

Faithfully,
John J. Pershing
Commander-in-Chief

[54]

G. H. Q.

AMERICAN EXPEDITIONARY FORCES,

General Orders
No. 38-A.

France, February 28, 1919.

MY FELLOW SOLDIERS:

Now that your service with the American Expeditionary Forces is about to terminate, I can not let you go without a personal word. At the call to arms, the patriotic young manhood of America eagerly responded and became the formidable army whose decisive victories testify to its efficiency and its valor. With the support of the nation firmly united to defend the cause of liberty, our army has executed the will of the people with resolute purpose. Our democracy has been tested, and the forces of autocracy have been defeated. To the glory of the citizen-soldier, our troops have faithfully fulfilled their trust, and in a succession of brilliant offensives have overcome the menace to our civilization.

As an individual, your part in the world war has been an important one in the sum total of our achievements. Whether keeping lonely vigil in the trenches, or gallantly storming the enemy's stronghold; whether enduring monotonous drudgery at the rear, or sustaining the fighting line at the front, each has bravely and efficiently played his part. By willing sacrifice of personal rights; by cheerful endurance of hardship and privation; by vigor, strength and indomitable will, made effective by thorough organization and cordial co-operation, you inspired the war-worn Allies with new life and turned the tide of threatened defeat into overwhelming victory.

With a consecrated devotion to duty and a will to conquer, you have loyally served your country. By your exemplary conduct a standard has been established and maintained never before attained by any army. With mind and body as clean and strong as the decisive blows you delivered against the foe, you are soon to return to the pursuits of peace. In leaving the scenes of your victories, may I ask that you carry home your high ideals and continue to live as you have served—an honor to the principles for which you have fought and to the fallen comrades you leave behind.

It is with pride in our success that I extend to you my sincere thanks for your splendid service to the army and to the nation.

Faithfully,

John J. Pershing

Commander in Chief.

OFFICIAL:
ROBERT C. DAVIS,
Adjutant General.

Copy furnished to

Commanding.

Letter written by General Pershing to the soldiers under his command after The Great War (JC)

Certainly a letter like this would have warmed the heart of a veteran and made his service feel even more worthwhile. John Corzine was encouraged toward service by this example.

[55]

The 7th Cavalry's band adopted *Garryowen* as their marching tune and this gave the Seventh their nickname among the rest of the Army. *Garryowen* is a lively Irish tune that translates from the Gaelic as "John's Garden." The first known use of the tune was in the late eighteenth century, when it was a drinking song of rich young fellows in Limerick, Ireland who enjoyed a good time in the pubs.

Seventh Cavalry insignia

Corzine trained with "Terrible Terry" – Major General Terry de la Masa Allen, Sr. Allen was a decorated World War I veteran who commanded the 1st Infantry Division in North  Africa and Sicily from May 1942 until August 1943. He was later selected to lead the 104th Infantry Division as divisional commander. In his career, Allen earned two Army Distinguished Service Medals, a Croix de Guerre, a Silver Star, a Legion of Merit, and two Purple Hearts. In May 1942, five months after the Japanese attack on Pearl Harbor, Allen was promoted to the rank of major general and given command of the 1st Infantry Division. "Allen's brash and informal leadership style won him much respect and loyalty from the men in his division, who wholeheartedly adopted his emphasis on aggressiveness and combat effectiveness rather than military appearances."

William Richardson, a career soldier, said this about the 7th Cavalry band and life at Fort Bliss before the draft began:

For the most part, Army training before the draft and World War II was very leisurely. Wednesday afternoons we were usually off duty and the officers played polo. We were off on weekends except for an occasional barracks inspection but if you stayed in the barracks, you were called out to water the horses morning and evening. Our regular training continued to be mounted in the morning and dismounted drill in the afternoon.

The 7th Cavalry had a mounted band assigned to the regiment and the band added so much to the esprit de corps of the regiment. The band was included as part of the Headquarters Troop. The army in 1940 did not mind at all if soldiers were fat. Most of the band members were fat and I don't think there were any two of them of the same nationality with the exception of probably some Indians out of the same tribe. The band was a motley crew but they were excellent musicians and were certainly an asset to the regiment. The bass drummer, a large Indian, was probably the fattest in the band. When they were mounted, he had a big drum on each side of him and all you could see of the horse was his neck and head in front and his hind end and tail in back.

We had a dismounted regimental parade about once a week, usually for Retreat, and they were always colorful and attended by family members and spectators. The 7th Cavalry band added to the precision marching that was expected of every trooper. Boots were always

[57]

highly polished and spurs gleamed in the evening sun. Garryowen had been the regimental song since the days when General Custer commanded the 7th Cavalry. When the band played it you could just feel the pride that everyone had for serving in a regiment with such a long and famous history.

Thus, Corzine provided a useful and important function for the morale of the troops by "wailing away" on his clarinet.

Presumed to be band members and girlfriends or wives (Corzine is front row, left) (JC)

Fort Bliss (from Christmas dinner menu, 1940) (JC)

**Front cover of Easter morning service, 24 March 1940,
Fort Bliss (JC)**

The Easter Morning Service

March 24, 1940

9:45 A. M.

ORDER OF WORSHIP

ORGAN PRELUDE—"*Melody in F*"............................Rubenstein

* PROCESSIONAL HYMN—"*Christ the Lord Is Risen Today*" No. 63

* A Call To Worship

* Invocation (To be said by all)

> *Almighty God, unto whom all hearts are open, all desires known, and from whom no secrets are hid, cleanse the thoughts of our hearts by the inspiration of Thy Holy Spirit, that we may perfectly love Thee, and worthily magnify Thy Holy Name, through Jesus Christ our Lord.* —AMEN.

* DOXOLOGY ....No. 252

RESPONSIVE READING—"*Christ's Resurrection*"............Page 319

* GLORIA ....No. 251

ANTHEM—"*Christ Arose*"................................Lowery
The Junior Choir

SCRIPTURE LESSON—Matt. 28: 1-9

MORNING PRAYER—LORD'S PRAYER

CHORAL RESPONSE—

* HYMN—"*In the Cross of Christ I Glory*"..............No. 61

ANNOUNCEMENTS—

ORGAN MEDITATION—"*Song Without Words*"............Thome

ANTHEM—"*Open the Gates of the Temple*"............Knapp
The Chapel Choir

SERMON—"*The Living Christ*"

SOLO—"*The First Easter Morn*"......................Wesley
Pfc. J. W. Fleeman

* RECESSIONAL HYMN—"*The Day of Resurrection*"............No. 62

* BENEDICTION—

* RESPONSE—

* POSTLUDE—"*Largo*" ....Handle

* The Congregation Will Please Stand.

**First page of Easter morning service, 24 March 1940,
Fort Bliss (JC)**

[60]

THE CHAPEL CHOIR

Organist
MRS. JEAN STILSON

Choir Director
MRS. ROBERTA R. SUNDT

Mrs. R. O. Wulfsberg
Miss Mildred Baird
Miss Frances Driver

Mrs. Hazel Hastings
Mrs. Brazilia Parker
Mrs. Harvie Ellis

Miss Frances Hall

Lt. H. S. Sundt
Lt. J. C. Damon
Lt. Carl B. Stilson
Lt. W. T. Weissinger
Pvt. O. Bulsterbaum
Pfc. J. W. Fleeman
Cpl. F. M. Burton

Pvt. G. Bueltermann
Pvt. G. Gersowitz
Pvt. W. Strausser
Pvt. P. McIntyre
Pfc. L. Dodge
Pvt. R. Nance
Pfc. V. Rux

THE JUNIOR CHOIR

MRS. HAZEL HASTINGS, *Director*

Lucy Serby
Lydia Allen
Nancy Allen
Peggy Voiles
Mildred Cook
Betty Stewart
Frankie Nagle

Mary Parrish
Jewel Fitzgerald
Georgianna Nagle
Marjorie Murray
Lorna May Smith
Rosalie Stewart
Caroline Ladue

Betty Rowe

CHOIR REHEARSALS

Junior Choir .... Wednesday, 4:30 P. M.

Chapel Choir .... Wednesday, 7:00 P. M.

ROY H. PARKER, Chaplain U. S. A.
Quarters No. 22—Telephones: Qts. 633, Off. 520

USHERS

The ushers for today are:

Pfc. J. Carzine   Pvt. D. D. Marbut

**Second page of Easter morning service, 24 March 1940,
Fort Bliss (Corzine's name is at left bottom) (JC)**

[61]

Cover of program, Christmas dinner, 1940, Fort Bliss

SEVENTH CAVALRY BAND

WARRANT OFFICER
Herman Webel

STAFF SERGEANT
Rosillo, Joe E.

SERGEANTS
Bobadillo, Candelario
Comasack, Frank
Evans, Thomas N.
Vallo, Romero

TECHNICAL SERGEANTS
Croteau, Lionel J.

CORPORALS
Horton, Robert L.
Stratton, Wilbur C.

PRIVATES FIRST CLASS
Smith, Tom B.
Bobadillo, Gregorio
Bryant, George D.
Corona, Hermogenes
Corona, Jesus
Corzine, John S.
Cravens, Theodore R.
Dumlao, Rufino D.
Enos, Andrew

Fleeman, John W. Jr.
Gonzalez, Francisco F.
Grie:, Charles
Hinojosa, Mateo
Lopez, Manuel
Molel, Rafael
Rodriguez, Feliciano
Rivero, Peregrine
Ruiz, Jose
Schoole:, William L.

Singleton, Scott R.
Wolders, Johonnes

RECRUITS ASSIGNED
Vance, Vedo
Wo:dag, John S.

ATTACHED
Cook, Garland A.
King, Charles H.
Mathews, John A.
Mathias, Robert C.
Nelson, Irwin
Hun:, Clarence E.
Erickson, John F.
Sandoval, Paul R.

Close-up of Corzine's name listed under Privates First Class
(JC)

[62]

HEADQUARTERS AND SERVICE TROOP
SEVENTH CAVALRY
FORT BLISS, TEXAS

CAPTAIN	FIRST LIEUTENANT	SECOND LIEUTENANTS
Walter E. Finnegan	John S. Little	Dennis L. Barton
COMMANDING		William M. Delaney
		Dee Harper

MASTER SERGEANTS
Cumarelas, John
Johnson, Walter
Smythe, Lester A.

TECHNICAL SERGEANT
Johnson, William
Schwartz, Benjamin

FIRST SERGEANT
Leonard, Joseph M.

STAFF SERGEANTS
Castelli, Carlo J.
Slagle, Marion A.
Urich, Russell

SERGEANTS
Adams, Earl H.
Boles, Arthur B.
Campbell, James J.
Christy, Arthur

SERGEANTS
Hora, Fred T.
Mace, Herman A.
McCormick, William J.
Nicholson, Malcolm E.
James J. Porter
Tittle, Joel C.
VanTill, ohn H.
Wiley, James
Wool, James P.

CORPORALS
Breuning, Clarence A.
Cory, Thomas M.
Lee, Charles S.
McClure, Dallas A.
Russell, Woodrow W.

PRIVATES FIRST CLASS
Allen, Hilton J.
Alexander, Lloyd E. Jr.
Ballard, Reuben G.
Bingham, Thomas J.
Bingham, Thurman F.
Black, Eugene R.
Bowden, Thomas E.
Butler, Omer
DeVore, James E. Jr.
Disney, Lawrence

Farley, David J.
Grofa, John W.
Hailey, Paul M.
Haislip, James B.
Harp, Ocie E.
Hemphill, Charlie O.
Hicks, Al W.
Kemp, William A.
King, George
Kilgore, Odis H.

Lawrence, Andrew
Larson, Einar F.
McClure, Wilson H.
Mehurim, Seth W.
Moss, C. B.
Reynolds, Stewart
Richardson, William A.
Sanders, William R. Jr.
Slater, Kenneth R.
Teer, James B.

Thompson, Grover
Vieres, Woodrow W.
Vinson, Escoe R.
Wawrzonek, Mitchell
Williams, Granklin
Williams, Oscar L.
Willis, Charles P.
Wittje, Henry J.
Wolf, Charles T.
Wrigh, Jim M.
Young, Eugene D.

PRIVATES
Abeyta, Gloyd
Anderson, James B.
Bearson, Fay H.
Begley, Alvin E.
Biggs, George D.
Black, Robert
Carbonatto, John
Carrillo, Victor Jr.
Carroll, Thomas J.
Christie, Ernest McG.
Clements, Merle M.
Coleman, Arthur J.
Cooper, Louis J. Jr.
Crespin, John A.
Curtis, Clayton R.
Davenport, Millard E.
Decker, Phil H.
Deighton, Lawrence R.
Dobbs, Silas M.
Dojaquez, Frank E.
Dunn, Willard H.
Eustice, William K.
Ferguson, Johnny E.
Ferguson, Lundy E.
Flint, William
Garcia, Felizardo S.

Gay, Henry C. Jr.
Glenn, Kenneth L.
Gobar, Robert A.
Goins, Carl B.
Grimm, William C.
Greywatch, Bennie
Hand, Nathan E.
Hand, Virgil L.
Harvey, Bob B.
Haug, Loren D.
Hayes, Robert T.
Herring, Claude L.
Hudgins, Bennie W.
Jackson, Leonard M.
Jamison, Neil
Johnson, James C.
chnson, Walton T.
ones, Jay L.
Kenney, ohn R.
Kintz, Byrel K.
LaGrange, Judd
Lane, Henry A.
Linsley, Radford J. Jr.
Lurance, Ray N.
Madril, Ernest
Mar, Paul K.

Martin, Tommy G.
Martinez, Joe L.
Martinez, Vaudello A.
McGlohen, Kenneth M.
McLeroy, Robert R.
Mitchell, Roy E.
Montana, Robert
Moore, Chester B.
Morgan, Roland O.
Nosby, Charles F. Jr.
Muffley, John H. Jr.
Munsell, William E.
Murphy, Walter W.
Myers, Walter W.
Phillips, Ervin
Prine, Calvin H.
Quesada, Hose A.
Ridley, Elmer L.
Proctor, Perry E.
Solyman, Gorge E.
Sanders, Milte M.
Stevens, Clifird W.
Sarvez, Jhn A.
Stringfellow, Ben S.
Terry, Evan L.

Timmons, William A.
Toellner, Harold L.
Turman, Jesse B.
Valehzuela, Guadalupe
Valenzuela G. S.
Vineyard, Willie A.
Walker, George E.
Weir, Wayne C.
Wemsauer, Edward N.
Wilcoxon, Joseph
Wrigh, William H.
Bake, James D.
Bush, John
Bradley, Durward S.
Coleman, Clair C.
Divendorf, Carl H.
Eberhart, Walter F.
Forrest, Benner M.
Harrison, James H.
Hignigh, Grover H.
Pharris, W. A.
Rowan, Charles A.
Navarro, Ralph
Todhunter, Robert J.
Yocum, John E.

SEVENTH CAVALRY BAND

WARRANT OFFICER	SERGEANTS	TECHNICAL SERGEANTS
Herman Webel	Bobadilla, Candelario	Croteau, Lionel J.
	Comasack, Frank	CORPORALS
STAFF SERGEANT	Evans, Thomas N.	Horton, Robert L.
Rusillo, Joe E.	Vallo, Romero	Stratton, Wilbur C.

PRIVATES FIRST CLASS
Smith, Tom B.
Bobadilla, Gregorio
Bryant, George D.
Corona, Hermogenes
Corona, Jesus
Corzine, John S.
Cravens, Theodore R.
Dumfao, Rufino D.
Enos, Andrew

Floeman, John W. Jr.
Gonzalez, Francisco F.
Griel, Charles
Hinojosa, Mateo
Motel, Manuel
Motel, Rafael
Rodriguez, Feliciano
Rivero, Peregrine
Ruiz, Jose
Schooler, William L.

Singleton, Scott R.
Woldors, Johannes

RECRUITS ASSIGNED
Vance, Vedo
Wo dag. John S.

ATTACHED
Cook, Garland A.
King, Charles H.
Mathews, John A.
Mathias, Robert C.
Nelson, Irwin
Hun, Clarence E.
Erickson, John F.
Sandoval, Paul R.

Headquarters Troop Band members on Christmas program 1940, Fort Bliss (JC)

[63]

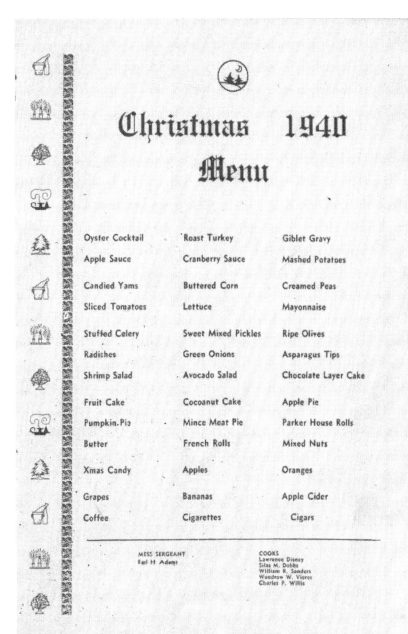

Christmas 1940
Menu

Oyster Cocktail	Roast Turkey	Giblet Gravy
Apple Sauce	Cranberry Sauce	Mashed Potatoes
Candied Yams	Buttered Corn	Creamed Peas
Sliced Tomatoes	Lettuce	Mayonnaise
Stuffed Celery	Sweet Mixed Pickles	Ripe Olives
Radishes	Green Onions	Asparagus Tips
Shrimp Salad	Avocado Salad	Chocolate Layer Cake
Fruit Cake	Cocoanut Cake	Apple Pie
Pumpkin. Pie	Mince Meat Pie	Parker House Rolls
Butter	French Rolls	Mixed Nuts
Xmas Candy	Apples	Oranges
Grapes	Bananas	Apple Cider
Coffee	Cigarettes	Cigars

MESS SERGEANT
Earl H Adams

COOKS
Lawrence Disney
Silas M. Dobbs
William R. Sanders
Woodrow W. Vieres
Charles P. Willis

Christmas dinner menu, 1940, Fort Bliss (JC)

[64]

About three years after John had joined the Seventh Cavalry, and with the war imminent, he was reassigned to organize the Army Air Force Band at Luke Field, seven miles from Glendale, Arizona, and fifteen miles west of Phoenix. Now Luke Air Force Base, the field was named after Second Lieutenant Frank Luke (1897–1918). Lieutenant Luke has a dramatic story: he is a posthumous Medal of Honor recipient and the number two United States ace in World War I. He was shot down at Murvaux, between Verdun and Stenay, France, on 29 September 1918, after he had destroyed three enemy balloons. Surviving the crash of his Spad biplane fighter aircraft, Lieutenant Luke drew two pistols and fired on German soldiers, killing several of them before he was killed.

Corzine (left front) playing with the Luke Field band, which he helped to organize (JC)

The first class held at Luke Field, with forty-five students, Class 41 F, arrived 6 June 1941 to begin advanced flight training in the AT-6 Texan. During World War II, Luke

[65]

Field was the largest fighter training base in the Army Air Forces, graduating more than 12,000 fighter pilots. The course of advanced flight training at Luke averaged about ten weeks and included both flight training and ground school. Approximately eighty hours of flying instruction covered topics such as formation flying, navigation, and instrument flying, as well as a bit of aerial acrobatics, which might come in handy in avoiding enemy aircraft, and aerial and gunnery training.

Ground school, as the classroom training for the advanced flying course was called, varied from about 100 to 130 hours and included instruction in navigation, flight planning, radio equipment, maintenance, and weather. On a typical day, cadets flew in the morning and attended ground school in the afternoons, or flew training missions in the afternoon after a morning of ground school. Thus, even if Corzine made friends with a pilot, the pilot would not there at Luke for very long. Likely, most of his friends were also band members.

The main gate at Williams Field, 1942
(just as Corzine would have seen it when he arrived)

Postcard from Williams Field

[67]

In June of 1942, after American had been at war for six months, John was sent to Williams Air Base to organize the 534th Army Air Force Band. Williams was located in Maricopa County, Arizona, east of Chandler, and about thirty miles southeast of Phoenix. The area has since been annexed by the city of Mesa, after the base closed in 1993. During World War II, Williams Field was under the command of the 89th Army Air Force Base Unit, AAF West Coast Training Center. Thousands of future P-38 Lightning pilots learned their twin-engine flying skills at Williams, where they trained in the Beech AT-10 Wichita. Williams began to offer four-engine training with Boeing B-17 Flying Fortress bombers in December 1944. The Army Air Forces also developed a pilot training program for the Chinese Air Force. The Air Corps conducted most of the

training for the Chinese at Luke, Williams, and Thunderbird Fields in Arizona. Both the small stature of the Chinese pilots and the language barrier were challenging for the program. Eight hundred and sixty-six Chinese pilots completed the training.

By the time John had been at Williams for two and a half years, in December of 1944, he had achieved a great deal. At twenty-three years of age, not only was he a First Sergeant, he was also married to Mary DeBons and had a baby son. **Photo: John Corzine (R) 1943. (JC)**

KEY MAN

The duties of an Army band's first sergeant are identical with those of any other "top kick" except that he has to "face the music."

For all that, First Sergeant John S. Corzine of the 534th AAF Band at Williams, has suffered no visible ill effects. In the two and one-half years that he has been stationed here he has acquired a permanent staff-sergeantcy, a wife, and a baby son—not a bad showing for a man of 23.

T/SGT JOHN CORZINE

[69]

John was born in Amity, Arkansas, but moved to the border town at an early age and lived there until the start of the war. He was a member of the high school band, playing the sax and carinet, and after school hours helped his father in the grocery store.

After graduating from high school in 1939, John joined the Seventh Cavalry Band at Ft Bliss, Texas—the same Seventh Cavalry made famous by Custer of "Custer's Last Stand." Sgt Corzine trained under General Terry Allen, one of America's famous fighting generals.

Three years later he joined with a cadre of three other men to organize the AAF band at Luke Field. In June, 1942, a similar mission brought him to Williams where he also helped start the band, and has remained ever since.

Of the vast number of things the band's key man finds himself sure of, one is what the sergeant will do after the war. The couple have definitely decided to return to Texarkana where John will go into business, possibly the grocery business, as he knows it best.

But, for an outside interest, he will always come back to his sax and clarinet, for, in the last few years these instruments have almost become second nature to him.

After his service in World War II, John Corzine moved to Detroit, where his wife Mary was from originally. Corzine pursued various careers during the rest of his life, including owning a Pure Oil gasoline station, driving a Detroit city bus, and working for the Detroit Street Railway. During this time in Detroit, his personal life did not work out as he might have hoped. Then, John moved to Florida and became a district manager for the 7-11 grocery chain.

**John Corzine with his father, Martin Corzine,
in Texarkana, 1970 (JC)**

In September of 1970, John re-married his first wife, Mary. She looks very hopeful in their photograph, but unfortunately, their new-found happiness was not to last very long. John passed away on the fourth of February, 1971, at only forty-nine years of age.

John and Mary at their re-marriage, September 1970 (JC)

John Studdard Corzine, who received encouragement to join the military from his father, also passed this legacy on to his son. John Ernest Corzine served our country in the Air Force from June 1962 until June 1966, continuing the proud Corzine family tradition. John trained at Lackland Air Force Base in San Antonio, Texas and spent a year at Keesler Air Force Base in Biloxi, Mississippi for technical training.

Lackland Air Force Base is the only entry processing station for enlisted Basic Military Training (BMT) for the active duty Regular Air Force, Air Force Reserve, and Air National Guard. Every airman passes through the "Gateway to the Air Force." Prior to 22 September 1993, Lackland's Medina Annex was also home to Air Force Officer Training School (OTS), which is now at Maxwell Air Force Base in Alabama.

John E. Corzine, 1962 (JC)

Lackland: "Gateway to the Air Force"

[73]

The name Keesler Air Force Base is synonymous with "training." During the Cold War, in late May 1947, the Radar School arrived on Keesler, making Keesler responsible for operating the two largest military technical schools in the United States. Keesler remained the largest training base up through the 1970s.

Keesler Air Force Base, 1980s postcard

In 1949, the Radio Operations School transferred to Keesler and in early 1956, Keesler entered the missile age by opening a ground support training program for the Atlas missile. In 1958, all control tower operator, radio maintenance, and general radio operator courses came to Keesler. Hopefully, even with all this time spent training, John was able to spend some time on that lovely Biloxi beach!

During his four years in the Air Force, John was part of the Strategic Air Command and maintained the SAC red phone at two base assignments: Columbus Air Force Base, located approximately nine miles north of Columbus, Mississippi and

Eglan Air Force Base, near Fort Walton Beach, Florida, where the Tactical Air Warfare Center was activated on 1 November 1963.

SAC was originally established in the U.S. Army Air Forces on 21 March 1946. An incredibly important command, the Strategic Air Command was responsible for Cold War command and control of two of the three components of the U.S. military's strategic nuclear strike forces, the so-called "Nuclear Triad," with SAC having control of land-based strategic bomber aircraft and intercontinental ballistic missiles or ICBMs. The third component was the submarine-launched ballistic missiles (SLBMs), operated by the Navy. SAC also operated all strategic reconnaissance aircraft, all strategic airborne command post aircraft, and all USAF aerial refueling aircraft, including those of the Air Force Reserve and Air National Guard. Thirty SAC B-52Fs were deployed to Andersen Air Force Base, Guam on 17 February 1965, representing the first delivery of SAC aircraft deployed for the Vietnam War.

Shield of the Strategic Air Command

A red phone, the primary alerting system in SAC Headquarters, on the desk of senior controllers, June, 1959 (National Security Archive, George Washington University.)

Some younger readers may not know what the "Red Phone" was. During the Cold War era, a red phone system, with dedicated connections to 200 operating locations internationally, supported communications in the SAC underground command post. The President of the United States is at the top of a chain referred to as National Command Authority (NCA) which is involved in the release of nuclear weapons. At one point there was a telephone/radio system that included the President and the senior officers at the North American Air Defense Command (NORAD) and at SAC. Three locations, SAC alternate command center at Barksdale Air Force Base, Cheyenne

Mountain, and Offutt Air Force Base, contained all of the communications links necessary to control all strategic elements of the armed forces. The Airborne Launch Control Center (ALCC) was in the air constantly, to launch ICBM's if the ground-based systems were destroyed. The ALCC staff knew the location of each person (in order of authority) and how to get in touch with them. There was a general on board who had a copy of the latest intelligence summary on Soviet strategic assets as well as the general world situation. If a call had to be made, the caller would work his way down from the President, to the Vice-President, to the Secretary of Defense, until he reached the appropriate person or until a certain time expired. The general on board had the launch codes needed to execute the Single Integrated Operating Plan (SIOP) or Limited Nuclear Option (LNO). (Michael Graham, Counterforensics, as cited in "Hotline Telephones - Making Sense of the Colours and Their Use" edited by Jerry Proc.)

This is what the red phone was for – launching a nuclear attack. It was no small job to maintain one of these red phone connections. The security of the Free World depended on it.

Columbus Air Force Base Barracks

[77]

Why was John sent to Columbus Air Force Base and not to Offutt Air Force Base, for example? It was because, during the 1950s, Strategic Air Command wings had become extremely large. As the Soviet missile threat became more pronounced and warning time of a Soviet launch decreased, these large Strategic Air Command bases presented increasingly attractive targets for enemy attack. By providing additional bases to which the aircraft could be dispersed, the enemy would have more difficulty in finding a target and more bombers could become airborne within a shorter period of time. Thus, SAC took over Columbus Air Force Base in April of 1955. The aircraft wings at Columbus took part in air refueling operations, trained in bombardment operations, and maintained a SAC nuclear alert posture.

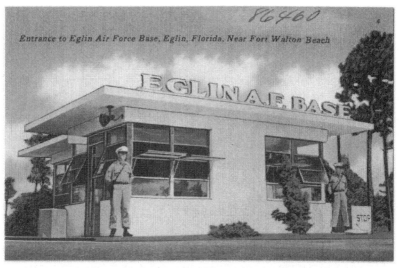

Postcard of Eglin Air Force Base entrance

John was next stationed at Eglin Air Force Base, the USAF Special Air Warfare Center was activated 27 April 1962. The center undertook to develop tactical air doctrine while training crews for special air warfare in places like Southeast

Asia. By mid-1963, SAW groups were in Vietnam and Panama. The USAF Tactical Air Warfare Center was activated at Eglin on 1 November 1963. With the increasing U.S. involvement in Southeast Asia in the 1960's, the need for increased emphasis on conventional weapons development made Eglin's mission even more important, and John was there protecting American freedoms. Once again, I hope he spent some time relaxing on the shimmering white sands of the Florida panhandle.

Jets over Fort Walton Beach

After his time of military service, John's first job was at Luke Air Force Base at Litton Industries working on the F104 inertial navigation systems. He had no idea his father had been stationed there during World War II. One could certainly say that in this case, "What goes around, comes around."

It has been an honor to share the story of three generations of Corzine men, all dedicated to preserving liberty. How grateful our nation is for men like these!

Colonel Raymond Irvin Brasaemle

Major in the 163rd Engineer Combat Battalion, WWII

Ray Brasaemle was born on 17 January 1912 in Akron, Ohio, to parents, John and Cora Cooley Brasaemle. John's grandfather was born in Germany, and his father was a merchant with a "5 & 10st store" in Akron. On the 1930 U.S. Federal Census, Ray was eighteen years old and a salesman in a store in Barberton, Ohio. He lived at home, and presumably, worked in his father's store.

Ray's father died before the war, in 1935. Ray didn't inherit the store, and he moved on after his father died. Ray married Retha May Richardson in Glasgow, Montana on the fifth of June, 1937.

Brasaemle enlisted in the U.S. Army on 1 July 1940, before World War II began. He wrote an unofficial history of the 163rd Engineer Combat Battalion in Europe while he was billeted in Austria in August of 1945 – before the war in the Pacific had officially ended and before he knew what the final outcome of the war would be.

An "engineer combat battalion" was a designation for a battalion-strength combat engineering unit in the U.S. Army. These battalions were a component of the United States Army Corps of Engineers. The battalions consisted of a headquarters and service company, three lettered companies, and a medical detachment. An ECB company consisted of company headquarters and three platoons. An ECB platoon consisted of platoon headquarters and three squads of thirteen men each. The normal work party was one squad with its own tool sets: a carpenter set, a pioneer set, and a demolition set, all transported in a 2-ton dump truck.

The *United States Government War Department Engineer Field Manual FM-5-5, Engineer Troops, 11 October, 1943*, stated that, "The mission of the engineer combat battalion of the infantry division is to increase the division's combat effectiveness by means of general engineer work." The ECB's

[82]

duties are most remembered as pontoon bridge construction, but there were other duties as well:

(1) Removal and passage of enemy obstacles, including mine fields and booby traps. (2) Preparation of obstacles by demolitions and other means, including laying mine fields and setting booby traps. (3) River-crossing operations to include use of assault boats, preparation of fords, and other stream-crossing expedients; and construction of vehicle ferries, portable bridges, and, in emergencies, pontoon bridges-capable of sustaining combat team loads. (4) Emergency repair and maintenance of roads, and reinforcement, repair, and maintenance of bridges. (5) Engineer reconnaissance. (6) Providing local security for own working parties.

b. Important duties less common than those given above are (1) Rapid general lay-out of rear positions, signs for marking routes, and guiding units to sectors. (2) Construction of fixed bridges and roads. (3) Construction, improvement, and maintenance of advance landing fields. (4) Defense of mine fields and other obstacles. (5) Combat as infantry. (6) In a stabilized situation, construction of the more elaborate defensive installations requiring the use of special engineer equipment, (7) Tank hunting.

Just as the army "moves on its stomach," it also must have roads and bridges on which to move.

In an emergency, the combat battalion fought as infantry, and their personal armament included "the bayonet, Carbine, rifle, and pistol." Supporting weapons included "caliber .30 and caliber .50 machine guns, caliber .45 submachine guns, antitank rocket launchers, and antitank rifle grenades."

Cover of Camp Van Dorn pamphlet

The 163rd Engineer Combat Battalion was activated on the fifth of May 1943, at Camp Van Dorn, Mississippi, near Centreville, at the lower southwestern edge of the state. Ray remembered Camp Van Dorn for its "state of semi-civilization." Roads had been carved out of jungle and pushed through swamps. The men spent their evenings there building duckboards in order to get around the camp. (Duckboards are a number of wooden slats joined together, placed so as to form a path over muddy ground.) Ray also didn't appreciate the heat in Mississippi: "What was a cool breeze at Van Dorn felt like something from a blast furnace. Hades itself couldn't have been much warmer." The barracks were constructed of tarpaper and heated by coal or wood heaters – heaters which Ray obviously thought the camp didn't need very badly.

Men came from Mississippi, Alabama, Tennessee, Louisiana, Georgia, Kentucky, New York, Washington, California, Michigan and New Hampshire to join the 163rd, and their training would begin on 1 June (1943). While waiting for training to begin, the men were not allowed to go into the nearby town of Centreville:

Downtown Centreville, 1944

[85]

Then there was Centreville, that lovely little spot where nobody could go. Passes weren't unheard of. Everybody heard of them, it was just that nobody ever got one. Centreville was off-limits, so we stayed in camp. And then the troubles, let us say misunderstandings, with our colored brethren were lessened. No, Van Dorn will not be forgotten so easily, although its memories weren't particularly pleasant.

This quote from Ray brings up another subject: the "Camp Van Dorn Slaughter," which was an alleged massacre of black soldiers occurring at the Camp Van Dorn Army installation. The alleged victims were members of the 364th infantry regiment, who had protested racial inequities on the base and in the surrounding community. The Army confirms at least half a dozen racial incidents occurred in the area, but denies the massacre ever took place. One soldier, Private William Walker, is confirmed to have died, having been shot by a local sheriff while escaping from MPs at the front gate. He was returning to base from R&R.

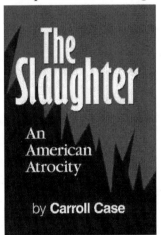

Ray says that passes being cancelled lessened the antagonism, which seems reasonable, as there would be fewer chances for trouble to start up if the men were confined to base.

A book, *The Slaughter: An American Atrocity* by Carroll Case, described a night in the fall of 1943 when white troops and military police armed with machine guns surrounded the 364th's barracks, and shot the African American soldiers "like fish in a barrel." The book claims that 1,227 soldiers were killed that night, which amounts to about a third of the regiment. Their bodies were reputedly loaded into rail cars and buried on the outskirts of the camp in trenches which were subsequently covered by a twelve-acre lake. The Army has displayed a series of aerial photographs of the camp and surrounding area taken since 1943 that show no such lake or any other signs of a mass grave. Although the NAACP has looked into the matter, "No hard evidence of the massacre has ever surfaced." (Washington Post.) Whatever actually happened, Captain Ray was there for it.

Men of an infantry regiment at Camp Van Dorn

Basic training was tough in the hot Mississippi sun, and the dispensary was always full. There were night maneuvers, calisthenics, close order drill, and grueling hikes in which the men had to make five miles in sixty minutes. The men also made bivouacs at Dixie Springs, and built pontoon bridges there and on the Red River in Louisiana. There were classes held under the "Big Oak," Saturday inspections by the Commanding Officer, and "nightly floor shows" – which meant scrubbing them until they gleamed!

Men attending outdoor service at Camp Van Dorn

There was a little recreation. There were movies, and at the Post Exchange a soldier could write a letter or listen to the radio. Most men had Saturday afternoon off as well as Sunday, but sometimes kitchen duty got in the way. One thing Camp Van Dorn had in its favor, though, was "the most beautiful sunsets you ever saw."

The 28th of August meant the end of Basic Training. Hoping to finally get a furlough, the men were disappointed to be sent to bivouac at Dixie Springs and then moved to the Louisiana Maneuver Area, about 250 miles away, on 15 September. Ray moaned:

> Thus began the Great Battle of Louisiana which had several interesting aspects. Bivouac areas were shared with the South's finest hogs. Movements were a signal for the heavens to open up with one of their special maneuver rainstorms. Winter came early to Louisiana that fall, or so it seemed at least, for the nights were cold – damned cold.

For the next nine weeks, the 163rd moved all across the maneuver area, crossing the Sabine River twice. This was the most difficult period the battalion had seen to date. A guard was set up on a two hours on/two hours off schedule, 24/7. The guard had to wear all his equipment while on duty. For the first two weeks, Company Able maintained the roads in the vicinity of Florien. These roads were not macadam, but plain dirt – alternatively dusty or muddy – and Able worked them in the dust, in the sun, and in the rain. Ray added that:

> Life was a nightmare of movements at night, fatigue, labor, and darn little to eat. At times there were only two scanty meals a day. The brass called it "conditioning" but the men called it "murder."

On the 24th of September, the company moved out and built a 25-ton capacity heavy pontoon bridge across the Sabine. Carrying the pontoon and trestle down a 70-degree angled, 150-foot slope was a challenging task. The most defeating part of the exercise was being ordered to take the bridge down the very next morning! It was during this difficult time, however, that Brasaemle was promoted to Major, so he was rewarded for his efforts.

When the unit returned to Camp Van Dorn on the seventeenth of November, it was "bitterly cold." All the men were thankful to see the "smokestacks and water towers of Camp Van Dorn once again." One squad barely made it back, as their truck was hit by a fast passenger train, the men having jumped out just in time.

Things were a little different for the men now: Centreville was no longer off limits, and the officers "beat a path to Baton Rouge [Louisiana] nightly." Company A, however, was sent to Sharonville, Ohio on the 21st, to work with steel trestle bridge equipage, testing the interchangeability of parts for a new prefabricated steel pier. The men were able to enjoy the female companionship of the town and catch a bus to Cincinnati – a twenty minute ride – if they had the fare, so the men definitely enjoyed this time period better than they had Basic or the Louisiana Maneuvers. Thanksgiving included the "nearest thing to a home-cooked meal the men would ever have in service," and steady girlfriends were invited. Many of the men had rented houses and had their wives visiting them.

December 7th found Company Able en route to Camp Van Dorn for Preparation for Overseas Movement (POM) training. This included such fun activities as infiltration courses through the ever-present mud; bivouacs in air-ground training in the bitter cold; classes in military censorship; machine gun qualifying tests, and the assault on the simulated wall on the outskirts of the camp. Then, of course, there was the highlight of the training: the twenty-five mile march. "After this hike the Company area looked like an invalid home – few indeed could walk without limping." After all this, the men got a short furlough.

On 20 February the 163rd, "fully girded and equipped," entrained for Camp Shanks, New York, their point of embarkation (POE). After a week of inspections, and hoping for a pass to see some of New York City, the Headquarters and Company A moved down the Hudson by steamer and boarded the SS *Christobal*, a converted luxury liner. Companies B and C followed the next day. On Sunday morning, the 27th of February 1944, the *Christobal* set sail across the Atlantic – and many of the men's complexions turned rather green as the ship began to roll.

Except for the guard duty – four hours on and eight hours off – and getting routed out of bed for boat drills, life aboard ship was not bad. "The meals were excellent – for those who could retain them in their intended place." The engineers entertained the nurses, played poker and monopoly, stood in lines at the PX, and practiced air raids on the twelve-day voyage.

SS *Christobal*

The ship passed through the Irish Sea and landed in Swansea, Wales on 9 March. The next day, the Battalion disembarked and then entrained for Fargo Tent Camp on the Salisbury Plain in Wiltshire – "the bleakest, coldest, windiest, and most barren spot in all England." I imagine that is precisely why this spot was chosen for such a large encampment of men.

After six days of orientation, inspection, and close order drill, where the men tried to get used to English money, weather, beer, and the blackout, the 163rd moved to Over Norton Camp near Chipping Norton, in Oxfordshire. There the men perfected their bridge building skills with speed and precision. A good many roads were built for "Farmer Brown." Mine-field work was also required. There were also some other incidents: a series of stolen geese skirmishes, and a misunderstanding with the "American Indians" (the black troops).

The 163rd was not needed for the Normandy Invasion. The men were still in England, living in pup tents and rolling their bedrolls every morning, then making practice landings in the afternoon, when the invasion occurred. On the 21st of June, the main body of the battalion arrived at the marshaling area on the southeastern coast of England. A severe storm struck the English Channel, carrying away the prefabricated docks on the American beaches. The storm whipped up the waters of the Channel to such a degree that they were unnavigable. For five days the men waited; playing ball, sleeping, and eating. Finally, on the 25th of June, the battalion boarded LST's (Landing Ship, Tank) at Weymouth. Able Company landed on Utah Beach at 2100 hours on Sunday, 26 June 1944 – D-Day plus 20.

There were a few mines to clear, and the detonations "scared the daylights out of everyone," but only a few bodies from the previous invasion still floated with the tide. Even so, the men were impressed with the seriousness of their mission. Bulldozers had cleared the beach of debris, and for miles all that could be seen were LST's dropping off men and supplies. Now was the real test as to the effectiveness of those long months of training in the swamps of Louisiana.

The first night, the men saw a brilliant display of flares and ack-ack over the beach. The next day, the 163rd moved to an area midway between Bricquebec and St. Sauveur-le-Vicomte. They had yet to encounter the enemy, but as they left the beach behind, the evidence of previous fighting became more obvious: rutted roads and fields, pock-marked by mine and shell; fire-blackened pill boxes; and disintegrated houses. The town of Port l'Albe appeared to have been "lifted in its entirety by some huge bomb and dropped as one huge heap of rubble." From dawn to dusk, the men patched, tarred, and tamped the ravaged road, and cleared the shoulders. The front lines were only six or seven miles away.

Company C moved to Cherbourg to clean up the dock area, and provided the battalion with countless barrels of

German tar, tar kettles, and a concrete mixer. The rest of the battalion remained at Blandamour for thirty-five days, becoming accustomed to the "vinegar-like cider which furnishes the liquid component of the French diet, and the French cognac, which is apparently a mixture of alcohol and nitroglycerin." The men also tried to learn some of the French language, and souvenir collecting was a major pastime. Company A spent some time building a prisoner of war stockade near St. Jores. Next, they were assigned the operation of a quarry near Lithaire on 22 July, and a week later the 163rd was producing gravel and crushed rock from two separate quarries.

Bridge built by the 163rd

The unit moved to the west of St. Lo, "an area which probably had more dead cows per acre and which had the foulest odor of any place in France." After this, the 163rd was transferred to the Third Army, and on the night of the 7/8th of August, the unit made its "famous midnight ride" eighty-five miles to Ernee. "Starting just before midnight and riding all night, we traveled southward through the territory that had just been liberated by General Patton's armored columns." The battalion was attached to the XV Corps in support of the 79th Infantry Division and the 5th Armored Division and pushed to the east of Le Mans to Monfort-le-Gesnois, nearer the front, where the men worked at filling road craters, removing obstructions from roads and mine removal.

On the 13th of August, the men moved to Origny le-Roux, just east of Mamers. Two C Company men were injured by a booby trap along the road shoulder. That day also brought Company A's first contact with the enemy. While bivouacked at Bonnetable, the Company was strafed while deployed in the woods. The force of about twenty-five German Focke-Wulf FW-190s that was shooting at them men was driven off by U.S. P-51s. "Many a latrine became a foxhole expedient, and gladly so." Able was strafed again on the 15th by a single aircraft. On the 16th, the Company moved farther back when an encounter with enemy units was imminent. The men of Able Company were continually strafed for the next few days as they deployed in an island of scrub trees about 150 yards by 50 yards – an easy target for the enemy. The .50 caliber machine guns on Able's trucks made a sufficient anti-aircraft battery.

Seven days after meeting the enemy for the first time, Companies A and B built their first bridge – across the Seine River – a 635 foot treadway bridge (a floating bridge having two tracks as a roadway). Aircraft patrolled the bridge during construction, and no enemy activity was encountered. Over a hundred enemy planes tried to take out the bridge over the coming weeks. Company A, acting as infantry, dug in near Till-sur-Seine to prevent isolated German forces from cutting through and escaping to Germany. Fortunately, no Germans were sighted.

Example of infantry support bridge

Example of pontoon bridge

Engineers assembling a Bailey bridge

Members of 234th ECB haul a tank across the Saale River

One night, when the battalion was camped in a wheat field, six men came walking down the road. They greeted the first guard with a "hello," as they passed by. He replied "hello" back, and took no notice. A few yards farther on, the same six men greeted three more men of the 163rd, and this time one of them was Major Brasaemle. Ray called out, "Are you French?" By this time another of the U.S. men, a colonel, had "stuck his face in that of the nearest stranger, and he jumped a foot and shouted, 'Cover 'em, these guys are Germans!'" The Germans turned out to be fully armed, even carrying a machine gun. Ray generously mentions that all the officers were "recovering from an acute case of being surprised, if not scared."

On August 31st, the 1st Platoon of A Company arrested forty-seven prisoners, while killing and wounding several others. Then the battalion began a series of long moves, as many as eighty or ninety miles each. On one of these, two men of the 2nd Platoon were lost while investigating a booby-trapped automobile.

In September, the men built several bridges, one of which was a large steel stringered, fixed bridge. The battalion also conducted minesweeping operations and road maintenance. As fall weather set in, the men of Able Company moved into a factory in the city of Luneville. After moving to Igney, the men ate turkey for Thanksgiving in the pouring rain and three inches of mud. Here they experienced their first artillery pounding, which continued for two nights with shelling at fifteen-second intervals. Due to the rains, a large stream had flooded the surrounding fields. The day after the artillery shelling ceased, a U.S. P-47 dropped a 55-lb bomb, narrowly missing the men's bivouac. Amazingly, the water absorbed the fragments and concussion from the bomb, and there were no casualties.

When the men moved to Hirschland, they found a still that produced "beaucoup" cognac. Able Company was assigned to erect and maintain an extensive array of road blocks to prevent the Germans from attempting to disrupt supply and communication. Others built several Bailey bridges near Rexingen. The 163rd's first Christmas overseas was spent in Rexingen where there was an operating church. The men were billeted in homes for the snow flurries of the season.

In the bitter cold, the men worked 24/7 on road blocks, crater charges, and preparing bridges for demolition in the vicinity of Wingen. Then, on the 4th of January 1945, the Germans broke through the lines. Men of Able Company were trapped in various locales by the enemy attack. Several men were trapped in cellars, and some were captured, only to be released when the town was recaptured by the Americans four days later.

After a short rest, work resumed. In the heavy snow, the engineers dug secondary defensive positions for the 398th Regiment, 100th Division. One and a half months were then spent on rebuilding a supply road which had become a quagmire. By the 17th of March, winter was letting up, and the unit moved to Rimling, sweeping the road shoulders for mines.

On the 18th, Company A moved to Ormersviller, a small town in Alsace, just over the line from Germany. Despite constant shelling, the unit moved into Germany on the 23rd of March. The men were to build a 970-foot treadway bridge across the Rhine River in support of the 3rd Division. "Working in a virtual sea of shrapnel, the men continued work regardless of the mounting casualties." Then a suitable road had to be built for the bridge approach. A P-47 flyover greatly helped matters.

As the German resistance began to crumble, the Germans began to destroy any bridges that would aid the advancing Allied armies. The 163rd had a big job to do, to build enough bridges to keep the army moving. A pile-driven fixed bridge was built across the Saale River at Bad Kissingen. This was the first time pile-driven bents were used. The difficult feat of building a fixed wooden bridge beneath a 90-foot Bailey bridge that was still in use was accomplished by the 1st Platoon of A Company, and then the Bailey bridge was disassembled, all without holding up traffic.

Engineers ferrying infantry soldiers in M2 Assault Boat

On the 26th of April, A Company encountered heavy shelling fire while ferrying materiel over the Danube River in support of the 42nd Division. The following day, the men built a 276-foot treadway bridge across the Lech Canal. Four prisoners were captured on the 29th of April. On 30 April, the battalion moved into Munich. Headquarters was set up in a city park, and the various Platoons occupied the buildings to which they were assigned. For four days, the men rested, wined, and dined at complete leisure, while "living in beautiful apartment houses and drinking champagne."

May 4th saw the battalion moving to the foothills of the Bavarian Alps, where they rested for four days. Then, the unit was moved to Teisdorf to start work on a bypass that led from

Munich to Salzburg. Next, the men moved to a small resort on a lake in the Salzburger Alps. After several days, the unit put tread on the last bridges near Trieste, and then guarded them. After this mission, Company A returned to Salzburg, Austria, where Ray Brasaemle finished his story.

While official documentation is not available for the 163rd Battalion, the 157th Engineer Combat Battalion spent the time after VE Day working with German prisoners of war and civilians on the restoration of utilities in Salzburg and repairing roads and railroads.

Veteran Donald Pruett says of the 163rd that, "We built a total of forty tactical bridges in France and Germany, including bridges over the Moselle, Meurthe, Rhine, Neckar, Main, Saale and Lech Rivers. We were in Salzburg, Austria, on VE day. The 163rd was disbanded after VE day and did not come home as a battalion. I landed in New York Harbor on Dec. 26, 1945."

Major Ray Brasaemle continued to serve his country by participating in the Korean War and in Vietnam. He was finally released from the U.S. Army on the seventeenth of January 1972, with the rank of Colonel. He died on 9 June 1983 in San Diego and was buried at Ft. Logan National Cemetery in Denver, Colorado, after years of proud service to his country.

Private First Class
Harold Lee Frank

Harold Frank, 357th Infantry, 2nd Battalion, Company G
(*The Davidson County Dispatch.*)

I met Harold Frank at a local veterans' event. After only a few minutes of conversation, it became apparent that he had a fascinating story to tell.

Frank was born on 30 September 1924 and grew up in rural Davidson County, North Carolina. He was the second oldest of five children born to Edward and Annie Wood Frank. As a farm boy, he learned early to shoot and enjoyed the sport. One year, a neighbor paid him a nickel for every blue jay he killed from the man's pecan trees, which was a fun way for Harold to earn a little spending money. His love of shooting would affect his choices when he joined the Army.

His family rented crop land and grew both cotton and sweet potatoes. Like most parents of this time period, his parents were loving, but strict with the children and each child had chores to accomplish.

Frank graduated from high school in 1942. The family had a good crop of sweet potatoes his senior year and he was able to use some crop money to pay for his cap and gown at graduation. Money was tight for rural farmers in the 1930s and 40s, as they slowly pulled out of the Depression era.

Harold got a job at the North Carolina Finishing Company in Salisbury after high school, and when he came home at night from work, he would help his mother with his younger siblings. For those who are unfamiliar with the furniture industry, "finishing" is the final step of the manufacturing process that gives wood surfaces desirable characteristics, such as an enhanced appearance and increased resistance to moisture.

Almost a year after graduation, in 1943, Frank got his draft notice. His father instructed him not to join the Marines, and since he couldn't swim, the Navy was not a good choice, either, so he joined the Army, formally enlisting on 27 April 1943. He boarded a bus headed for Camp Croft, South Carolina. Frank says he learned his first war-time lesson on that bus, when an older recruit tricked him in a card game, but then kindly didn't take his money. "I know you ain't never been nowhere," was the older recruit's reason for his kindness. Frank learned an important lesson and never forgot it. That ten dollars he almost lost was all the money he had.

Soldiers at Camp Croft

Camp Croft

After Basic Training, Harold got a two-week pass to go home. He stood up on a bus all the way home to North Carolina. Frank made $50 a month in the Army. He sent $18 home to his mother each month, and told her to spend it to make her and his father's life a little easier. She never spent any of it. When Frank finally made it home, all the money was in the bank – in his name. In Harold's phrasing, "that was the kind of momma" he had.

Close-up view of barracks

Barracks inspection

Camp Croft entrance

Empty Mess Hall

Full Mess Hall

Every squad in the Army Infantry had one man who shot the Browning Automatic Rifle and Frank volunteered to shoot the BAR – which could explode with 400 rounds a minute of firepower – as he had grown up shooting and liked to shoot. He later felt that he hadn't known what he was getting into. I am sure that could be said of many young men as they entered service! Frank qualified quite highly with the rifle and could take it apart and put it back together blindfolded.

The Browning Automatic Rifle M1918 was chambered for the .30-06 Springfield rifle cartridge and designed by John Browning in 1917 for the U.S. Expeditionary Corps in Europe. The BAR, as the rifle was commonly referred to, was designed to be carried by infantrymen during an assault or advance while supported by the sling over the shoulder or fired from the hip. The U.S. Army, in practice, however, used the BAR as a light machine gun, often fired from a bipod. The BAR was issued as the sole automatic fire support for a twelve-man squad, and all men were trained at the basic level how to operate and fire the weapon in case the designated operator was killed or wounded.

**6th Marine Division at Okinawa
with the lead Marine carrying a BAR**

Harold had qualified for officer training, but turned it down because he was ready to "get over there and kill some Japs or Germans," a sentiment so many young men felt. He was sent to Fort George G. Meade, Maryland, where he trained with gas masks, and volunteered to be qualified with the M1 rifle. During World War II, Fort Meade was used as a recruit training post and prisoner of war camp, and it was also a holding center for approximately 384 Japanese, German, and Italian immigrant residents of the U.S. who were arrested as potential fifth columnists. Now the installation includes the Defense Information School, the Defense Media Activity, the United States Army Field Band, the headquarters of the United States Cyber Command, the National Security Agency, the Defense Courier Service, and the Defense Information Systems Agency.

Frank had never used a telephone, and his parents didn't even have one, but Frank managed to call his sister in Lexington to tell the family he was being sent overseas. He got quite a surprise the next day, when he was called in to see one of his officers. Wondering why he was in trouble, he was delighted to see his parents in the room. The Army allowed him the day off, and he and his parents toured Washington, D.C. This was a very nice send-off before he went overseas.

It was lucky that Harold had not joined the Navy, because in March of 1944, when he was onboard ship, headed across the Northern Atlantic to Scotland, he got sick before he lost sight of land and was sick all the way across. He says that when he arrived on land again, he got down and kissed the ground. He was just not cut out to be a sailor.

Frank was entrained down into England, there to train for the D-Day invasion. He landed on Utah Beach with the 357th Infantry Division. The *Regimental History of the 357th Infantry* says that:

> On this day, the battalions entrained, traveled 30 miles to Cardiff, Wales, and embarked on two ships, the SS *Explorer* and the SS *Bienville*. At 0730 of the 5th, the ships sailed down the River Severn and dropped anchor in the Bristol Channel near Swansea, where the convoy assembled. By 0200 of the 6th, the convoy was

underway toward France, following a route close to the coast of England. At this very moment, other men, many thousands of them, were "sweating out," the few remaining hours before they were to make the greatest assault landing in history...

At 0930 of the 8th, the convoy dropped anchor off Utah beach on the Cotentin Peninsula. Debarkation into big LCI's began at 1200 and by 1245 the first elements of the Regiment, led by Colonel Ginder, were wading ashore. At this time, the Regimental Commander was notified that the prearranged transit area had not yet been secured by the 4th Division – which had made the initial D-Day assault landing – and that the Regiment would move instead into an area in the vicinity of Loutres.

Frank had injured his knee and it hurt, but that did not deter him from digging a foxhole with another soldier. They dug in two-hour shifts. They were pleased with their three-foot deep foxhole until the shells started hitting nearby. Then they began digging again, and their foxhole was chest high when they were finished. In four days of combat, by the end of the 13th, the Regiment had suffered a total of 703 casualties. For three days and nights, Frank stayed in his foxhole, but the invasion had stalled and the commanders needed to know why. Harold was sent on the patrol to discover the reason for the delay.

During this patrol, Frank slid down a dirt embankment and landed on a German soldier. He reacted instinctively, stabbing the soldier, only to realize that he was already dead. It was 4 July before Harold got to take a bath and get a hot meal.

Three days later, Frank, with his unit, was crossing a road, dodging gunfire, and firing back. Suddenly, he felt a sharp pain in his shoulder. It felt like he had been kicked by a horse –

a stunning blow. After a few seconds, he realized he'd been shot. The men fought for nine hours and when they ran out of ammunition, the group attempted to cross a field (another account says "ravine") the Germans had flooded. Frank tried to

swim, giving away his BAR because he couldn't carry it due to the injury. When he came out of the water, he and his fellow soldiers were greeted by a German with a machine gun – which incidentally had more firepower than the BAR. The jig was up. It was 8 July 1944 and Frank and about 200 others were now the captives of the ruthless German 16th Parachute Division.

The next day, Harold was interrogated by a German officer, who had noticed his German-origin last name. He told Frank that he was fighting against his own ancestors. Frank calmly told him that his ancestors were from Tyro, North Carolina. Harold had carried his grandfather's pocket watch with him to war. When the interrogating officer demanded it, Frank let it fall to the floor while handing it over. The German officer kicked the broken watch, but allowed Frank to pick it up and put it into his pocket.

(Photograph: Paratroop Captain Walter Gericke.)

For the next few weeks, Frank and other captured American soldiers were marched at night across France and into Germany. They hid during the day, taking refuge in barns or stables. Although ordered to hold his hands up in the air, Frank was allowed to put his hand on his head. If the Germans had realized he was wounded, he might have been shot then and there. Those who couldn't march were killed and just tossed on the side of the road, like so much excess garbage.

After what seemed an eternity, the prisoners arrived at Stalag IVB, a prisoner of war camp located about thirty miles north of Dresden, Germany. IVB was the largest German POW camp, housing more than 20,000 POWs. Infection set in on Harold's shoulder and he began to be fearful of his chances of survival. Another American prisoner was a medic and he doctored Frank's infected shoulder. Frank credits him with saving his life.

Entrance to Stalag IVB

[111]

Main street in Stalag IVB

Watchtower at Stalag IVB

[112]

POWs at Stalag IVB

Despite the grueling hardships of life as a prisoner of war, there were little glimmers of kindness spread out amongst the depressing days. Frank volunteered to work in a paper mill, hoping it would be a slightly better living experience. He was transferred to the mill and worked twelve hours a day, seven days a week. He did get better food and a better place to stay, so it was worth the transfer.

Ever practical, a German doctor finally removed the bullet from Harold's shoulder because it limited his ability to work. It had been three months and eight days since he had been shot – Friday, 13 October 1944. When the doctor dropped the bullet in a dish, Frank asked the doctor for the bullet in his limited German vocabulary. The doctor gave it to him, and Harold has worn it around his neck many times over the years.

In an act of kindness, a foreman at the mill took Frank's grandfather's broken pocket watch, and a few days later, a guard returned the watch to Harold, with a repaired glass crystal. Frank still has that pocket watch.

At times, the men could hear the U.S. Air Forces bombing close by. A guard gave the prisoners some paint, and at night, they went on top of the barracks and painted "POW" in large letters on the roof. This was another act of kindness shown the men. This act could have definitely have been one that saved their lives. Bombs fell heavily on Saturday night, 11 April. When the bombing ceased, every building was on fire except the prisoner barracks. The pilots must have seen the message on the roof. Stalag V-A, near Ludwigsburg, actually had the roofs of the buildings within the camp marked "KG" for "Kriegsgefangenen," the German word meaning "prisoner of war." Large red crosses were also painted on the roofs, to further ensure that Allied planes would not mistakenly target the camp. It is hard to know if the Allies would think this was a German trick, or if it was for real. "POW," however, painted on the roof in English, would have been a better signal for the U.S. pilots.

Despite the better food at the mill, Frank still lost weight. To supplement the meager diet, Frank used his rural GI know-how, and fashioned a sling shot out of a rubber tube, and a branch from a scrub tree. He used it to shoot the large rabbits he'd seen around the camp. How he got away with the Germans smelling the odor of boiling rabbit around his barracks is a puzzle. Perhaps it was the timing of Frank's confinement. In late April 1945, with the Russian troops advancing into Germany, the POWs were moved. On a bustling road crammed, with POWs and civilians, the prisoners marched for two days with no food or water and very little sleep. One hundred and seven prisoners had left the camp. The number dwindled down to seventy in those two days. The men were just too weak from lack of food to be able to stand the march.

However, the march gave Frank and a friend the opportunity to escape. They remained on the run for five days, hiding in barns in the day and traveling at night, stealing potatoes from fields for food. Once, they even convinced a German guard that they were not POWs, despite their clothes.

Thinking they had evaded recapture, he and his buddy made a critical mistake. When stopped only thirty yards away by another German officer, they interspersed English in their conversation, not realizing he understood every word. The officer promptly took them back to the POW group. One cannot imagine how sick inside the men felt about making such a costly mistake.

Then, incredibly, on 7 May 1945, the guards stopped marching and suddenly began changing into civilian clothes. They had gotten word the war was over and had no desire to continue anything they were doing. The German soldiers were absolutely ready to be civilians again.

So unexpectedly freed, the prisoners walked until they came upon a bakery in a German village. With a little German money, they bought every loaf of bread the bakery had and continued down the road, eating the bread. They were found by an American unit and taken to get a good meal. Finally! After ten months of suffering – a hot meal they didn't have to shoot and prepare themselves.

The men were airlifted to Camp Lucky Strike in France – Frank's first plane ride. General Dwight Eisenhower came to see the former POWs and took offense at a cook telling the men they could not have all they wanted of a particular food. Frank was able to eat to his heart's content. The General even found a telephone and allowed each of the former POWs to call home. What a phone call that must have been! Can one imagine the joy of a mother when she heard her lost son's voice once more?

His POW report lists the date of 21 July 1945 as his date of being "Returned to Military Control, Liberated or Repatriated." Frank was sent to an Army hospital in Tennessee to recover from the physical aspects of his ordeal as a POW. He had lost one hundred pounds. The hospital personnel fed him six times a day trying to build him back up. When he was released from the hospital, he went home to Tyro, still dealing with the physical and emotional wounds from the war – as all the men and women who participated in World War II had to do. **(Photo: Frank still wears his medals, dog tags, & bullet.** *Davie County Enterprise Record.***)**

Harold married Reba Mae McDaniel on October the 11th, 1947 and they moved to the Cornatzer community in Davie County. The couple share four children, three grandchildren and several great-grandchildren He went to work for RJ Reynolds and became a reserve deputy with the Davie County Sheriff's Office. He also helped found the Cornatzer-Dulin Volunteer Fire Department.

Frank is now the last living survivor from Company G, of the 2nd Battalion, 357th Infantry that landed at Utah Beach.

An Unknown Lieutenant in India

The Unknown Lieutenant
10th Air Force, China-Burma-India Theater

There he was – standing on the streets of Calcutta, India talking with an African soldier. Who was he? What was he doing on that day? Why did he send pictures to my mother, carefully identifying each one in a chatty manner as if they accompanied a letter in the same, friendly vein?

[117]

I have been unable to answer any of these questions. He was not any relative of my mother's that can be identified. No one in my mother's hometown has identified him either. Was he a boyfriend that I know nothing about? That's possible. Or, it could be that my mother just wrote to a serviceman, as many high school girls were requested to do in the war, to enhance the troops' morale.

Whatever his circumstances, and whoever he was, I decided that I would honor him here on these pages by recording the pictures that he sent back from the war. I know that these photographs were sent to the States during the war time period, because all are stamped on the back with the words: Passed by Army Examiner, US, 42515."

One reason I have for believing that he might have been a co-pilot, flying in a C-47 over the "Hump" – the Himalayan Mountains – is because one of the pictures was taken from the co-pilot's seat on a C-47. He made the comment on the back of the photo, "Took a chance on this one, I didn't think it would come out." One can see farmland in the foreground and a winding river in the background of the photo.

Another reason for believing the unknown Lieutenant was a pilot is the photo of a large palace complex that states on the back, "This is the Palace we stayed at – Pretty nice, too, right on the beach." I know of several instances where pilots were given leave time and they stayed in the finer homes or estates in various countries. I have never heard of this being the case with anyone else except commanding officers.

Right wing of a C-47
(Notice the blur of the propeller spinning.)

Palace where the Unknown Lieutenant stayed

Fountain in front of the Marble Palace

The Marble Palace

While in Calcutta, the young officer visited the Marble Palace. The Marble Palace is a palatial nineteenth-century mansion in North Kolkata. It is one of the best-preserved and most elegant houses of nineteenth-century Calcutta. The house was built in 1835 by Raja Rajendra Mullick, a wealthy Bengali merchant who collected works of art. The front of the house is Neoclassical in style and the open courtyards in more traditional Bengali style. Adjacent to the courtyard, there is a "thakur-dalan," or place of worship for members of the family, built in the style of a Chinese pavilion. The premises also include a garden with lawns, a rock garden, a lake, and a small zoo.

Main Street of Calcutta

Calcutta business – Coondoo & Company

[121]

Calcutta Market

Calcutta Post Office

One of the Lieutenant's friends "arguing with a taxi driver"
on the streets of Calcutta

Indian boy

on the

Calcutta streets

Jain Temple in Calcutta

Modern view of the Jain Temple (Santanu)

[124]

The note on the back of the photo of the Marble Palace fountain says, "Didn't tell you about it. Remind me – huh??" This note seems to indicate that there was definitely an ongoing relationship between the man who sent the pictures and the person receiving them.

Unknown Lieutenant (center) standing on the steps of the Jain Temple, Calcutta

[125]

The young Lieutenant also visited the Jain Temple while he was in Calcutta. The temple was built by a Jain named Rai Badridas Bahadoor Mookim in 1867, and the complex is subdivided into four temple areas. The temple is dedicated to Parshwanath, who was the 23rd Jain Tirthankar, and devout Jains from all over India visit it. The interior of the main temple is lavishly decorated with beautiful chandeliers and mirrors, and the floor is intricately paved with marble and embellished with exquisite floral designs. "Jainism is an ancient religion from India that teaches that the way to liberation and bliss is to live a life of harmlessness and renunciation. The aim of Jain life is to achieve liberation of the soul." (The BBC.) Followers of Jainism are called "Jains," a word which connotes "the path of victory in crossing over life's stream of rebirths through an ethical and spiritual life." (Encyclopedia Britannica.)

The next photographs were taken in Puri, India, which appears to have been a bustling place in the 1940s.

"The heart of Puri" with the local marketplace

"During a picnic in Puri. My friends in white sweat shirts, the rest are English boys."

"An Indian boy saying his prayers at Puri."

"The Jagannath Temple at Puri."

"One of the other Jagannath temples."

Puri is in eastern India, situated on the Bay of Bengal. Located in the state of Odisha, the town was under the British Raj from 1803 until India attained her independence in August of 1947. The highlight of the city is the 12th-century Jagannath Temple. It is one of the original Char Dham pilgrimage sites for Hindus. King Indradyumna of Ujjayani is credited with building the original temple in 318 BCE. The Jagannath Temple has been plundered eighteen times during its history by thieves who desired its treasures.

The temple is famous for its annual Rath Yatra, the chariot festival, in which images of the three main temple deities are hauled on very large and elaborately decorated carts. The Rathas (chariots) are huge, wheeled, wooden structures, which are built new every year and are pulled by the festival participants. The chariot for Jagannath is approximately forty-five feet high and thirty-five feet square and takes about two months to construct. Flower petals and other designs decorate the carts.

King Indradyumna of Ujjayani

Modern view of the Jagannath Temple (Shiva-Nataraja)

Sadly, this is all I have of the Unknown Lieutenant's story. Did he make it back home after the war? Did he marry, have children, a good job, and a happy life? At this point, no one knows. Maybe someday I can discover who he was, but until then, I am happy to record his wartime photographic memories and honor him for his service to his country.

Lieutenant Colonel
Ralph Easterling

Ralph Easterling (RE)
5th Air Force, 49th FG, 8th FS

[133]

Ralph Easterling was born in Hartsville, South Carolina in 1924. Hartsville is the largest city in Darlington County, and yet the population was only 7,764 on the 2010 census. Hartsville was begun by Thomas Edward Hart, who came to the area in 1817 and built a plantation along Black Creek. James Lide Coker played a vital role in Hartsville's development. He and his family developed a seed company, an oil mill, a fertilizer plant, and the iconic J.L. Coker and Company General Store, housed in an impressive brick storefront, which even today remains a downtown landmark. The Cokers also created Welsh Neck High School, the forerunner of Coker College, and the Southern Novelty Company, the predecessor of Sonoco Products Company, a major provider of packaging and industrial products. (Hartsville Visitors Center.)

J.L. Coker and Company building in Hartsville

Ralph's father was a mail carrier who walked throughout the town delivering mail. Thus, the family was provided for doing the Great Depression. His grandfather was a master machinist who made spools and other items for the textile industry. Ralph had two older brothers, "who let me live," as he put it.

His brothers made such a name for themselves in sports that Ralph never felt he could compete. The two oldest brothers were actually half-brothers who had lost their father after a cotton gin accident, whose aftereffects included pneumonia. Ralph and the brother just older than himself shared a father.

Unfortunately, his mother developed crippling arthritis after Ralph's birth. Because of his mother's arthritis, the she and the children spent the summers up in the mountains in East Flat Rock, South Carolina, near Hendersonville. Ralph attended high school in the neighboring community of Old Flat Rock.

Example of a South Carolina bog with standing water

The community of East Flat Rock developed east of the Flat Rock community; and it was named East Flat Rock in the early 1900s to distinguish the two communities. Before development, it was an area of bogs and wetlands, with numerous small creeks flowing into Bat Fork Creek, which then flows into Mud Creek. Mountain bogs form in poorly drained depressions or on gentle slopes in relatively flat valley bottoms. This particular mountain bog was close to an ancient Indian path, the Saluda Path, which was part of the Cherokee Path that led from the Overhill towns of the Cherokee to Charleston, South Carolina, extending for 500 miles.

The community was sparsely settled prior to the early 1900's. The area was unsuitable for farming until machinery was invented in the late 1800s that could drain the bogs. The Southern Appalachian bogs are among the rarest natural habitat communities in the Appalachian Mountains, and are home to rare plants, reptiles, amphibians, and birds, such as the bog turtle, the mountain sweet pitcher plant, the swamp pink, the Gray's lily, the green pitcher plant, and the bunched arrowhead. (Hendersonville Heritage.)

Since where Easterling lived was almost "a stone's throw" from the Hendersonville Airport, Ralph spent all his spare time there. The airport was merely a sod strip, one of few in the mountainous terrain, but it was an exciting place for a young boy. He did any odd jobs he was able after school and on the weekends. In 1933, at age nine, he was given the chance to ride in a Ford Tri-Motor aircraft, and since that time, flying had become a passion for him.

Nicknamed "The Tin Goose," the Tri-Motor is an American three-engined transport aircraft. Production started in 1925 by Henry Ford and ended on 7 June 1933. A total of 199 Ford Tri-Motors were made. Its all-metal construction caused Henry Ford to claim it was "the safest airliner around." In the late 1920s, the Ford Aircraft Division was reputedly the "largest manufacturer of commercial airplanes in the world." This still held true during World War II, as the largest aircraft manufacturing plant in the world was built in Willow Run, Michigan, where Ford produced thousands of B-24 Liberator bombers under license from Consolidated Aircraft. (Jeanine M.

Head and William S. Pretzer. *Henry Ford: A Pictorial Biography*.)

FLY ═IN═ THIS FLY
Giant Tri-Motored Ford
14-Passenger All-Metal Airplane

GEO. KEIGHTLEY, 21 Years of Steady Flying   JOE MUSLEH, Stunt Flyer

1933   SPECIAL PRICES
July 27th, 28th, 29th and 30th
7 A. M. to 11 A. M., Rides 50c - 11 A. M. to 8 P. M., Rides $1.00

Scenic Trip over Mt. Pisgah $3.00
1-Hour Scenic Trip over Mt. Mitchell $5.00
2-Hour Scenic Trip over Smoky Mountains $10.00

THURSDAY - SATURDAY - SUNDAY
Parachute Jump and Stunt Flying

HENDERSONVILLE AIRPORT
Two Miles from Hendersonville on East Flat Rock Road

Easterling still has the advertisement for his never-forgotten ride in the Ford Tri-Motor (RE)

[137]

Easterling moved to Charlotte, North Carolina after he graduated from high school in 1941. Ralph mentioned there only being eleven grades in school when he graduated: "We were smarter than you folks!" I discovered during our interview that Ralph is a great kidder.

Easterling took a position at Terrell Manufacturing Company, which built textile-related machinery. His brother James had already arrived in Charlotte. Ralph's great uncle, John Kimbril, was part owner of the company, so a place in the company was waiting for Ralph. The Terrell Machine Company was incorporated the same month that the United States entered World War I, so that its president, E. A. Terrell, had to turn the office over to his wife just before he entered the army. During World War II, Terrell sponsored formation of a War Production Pool, which used the services of some twenty other firms to produce military equipment. (Charlotte Mecklenburg Library.) Sadly, as with almost all of the textile industry in North Carolina, the Terrell building on South Boulevard was abandoned in 1990, and the building was demolished in 1992.

When "things began heating up in Europe," Easterling told his mother that he was going to sign up as soon as the Army Air Corps began accepting men at age eighteen instead of age twenty-one. Of course, she said, "Hush!" No mother likes to think of her boy – especially her youngest – going off to war. However, on 18 November 1942, the draft age for the U.S. military was lowered to age eighteen, and Ralph signed up. He was called to active duty in February 1943.

Ralph's training went quickly and he had his wings in nine months, unlike the training replacement pilots received later in the war, which sometimes lasted twice as long, due to bottlenecks in the system. He came out with ten hours in the Curtiss P-40 Warhawk and seventy-two hours in the Republic P-47 Thunderbolt. This last were taken in Florida at Dale Mabry

Army Airfield, which had taken over the Dale Mabry Airport in Tallahassee. (It was returned to civilian use right after the war, in 1946.)

In October of 1940, hundreds of laborers began clearing swampland for temporary quarters for Air Corps personnel. The base became a nearly self-sufficient city, with several runways,

 barracks, officers' quarters, a mess hall, hangars, a hospital, a church, and a bowling alley. The field was activated on 13 January 1941. The first unit to train at Dale Mabry Field was the 79th Fighter Group, which was formed at the field in early February 1942 and equipped with Curtiss P-40 Warhawks. Over 8,000 pilots from Europe, China and the United States trained here in P-39s, P-40s, P-47s, and P-51s over the course of the war. Also, one hundred fifty German prisoners-of-war were housed at the Airfield in 1944 and 1945. **(Photo: Mabry Field, 1942.)**

When he was first learning to fly the P-47 Thunderbolt, Ralph frightened a few people. "The P-47 was lumbersome and heavy and you didn't feel the torque. One day I shoved the throttle forward and didn't get on the right rudder quick enough and it went veering off to the right toward the maintenance hangar. People were diving for cover!" he laughed. "I got yelled at by a few people after that."

Ralph with his mother, 1944 (RE)

Interestingly enough, in a typical government snafu, Easterling and his fellow pilots had been issued winter clothing before being sent to Mabry, so they were loaded down with heavy clothing for the 90 degree Florida days.

WAKDE AIRSTRIP - MARCH 1944
WAKDE ISLAND, PAPUA, N.G.

Next, Ralph was assigned to a place no cooler than Florida – to a grass air strip near Gusap, Papua New Guinea with the 5th Air Force, 49th Fighter Group, 8th Fighter Squadron. He had 290 hours of flying experience by the time he arrived in New Guinea. There he learned new skills such as "skip bombing": in Ralph's case, throwing bombs into caves in order to reach the Japanese troops hold up there. "When the terrain doesn't give it to you, you make it," he stated. He performed various missions, including dive bombing, strafing, fighter sweeps, and escorts. Close upon his arrival, a General called Easterling and the newest one hundred or so pilots to attention. He informed the men they would be flying P-40s. As a group, the men called out, "But, they're obsolete!" The General replied: "You didn't hear me, Lieutenants?" And the inevitable answer came: "Yes, Sir!"

Easterling was in combat for sixteen months, completing 120 missions, and spent the last six months in training others to go into combat. He was fortunate in that he never received a hit from enemy fire. Ralph said that he enjoyed flying, not fighting. He had one confirmed kill on a fighter sweep while flying a P-38, and three unconfirmed kills on his various missions. His planes did not have very good gun cameras: "They kept saying, 'there is a war going over in Europe' as the excuse for our outdated equipment."

On an early strafing mission looking for enemy shipping, Easterling made his dives and the ship – called a lugger – began to shoot back at him. "You're trained, but you don't really think about seeing that akk-akk from an enemy ship coming up at you," Ralph remarked. "You realized you're not shooting skeet. Someone's shooting at you."

½ MI. OFF PAPUA NEW
GUINEAS NORTH COAST

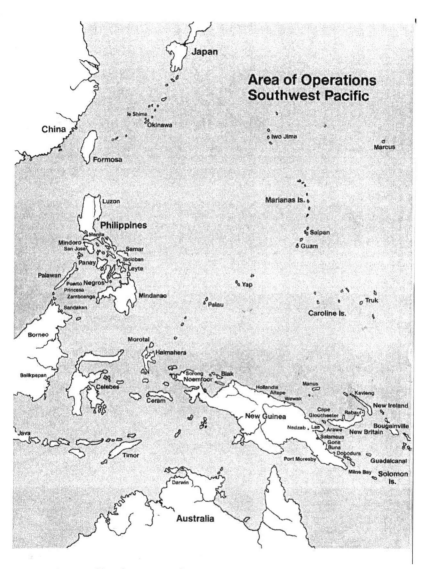

Easterling's map of the Southwest Pacific (RE)

"Poopy II" in Dobodura, New Guinea, May 1943

Flying Tiger ace David L. "Tex" Hill said of the Curtiss P-40 Warhawk:

"In the hands of a skilled pilot, the P-40 could exceed its limitations and could out-maneuver and out-fight anything in the sky. It was sturdy and handled well, except in a spin, but you never piloted a P-40 without wishing you had something a little better."

The P-40's performance was always regarded as inferior to German aircraft, specifically the Me-109 and Focke Wulf Fw-190, especially at altitudes above 15,000 feet. It could also be out-maneuvered and out-climbed by the Japanese Mitsubishi Zero. By 1944, when better fighters, such as the P-38 Lightning, P-47 Thunderbolt and P-51 Mustang, became readily available, the Warhawk was rendered obsolete. Nevertheless, many continued to be used in the South Pacific and China-Burma-India theaters right up until the end of World War II.

Easterling with his wings (RE)

Base Camp (RE)

Easterling in the cockpit of a P-38 (RE)

Gusap Airfield was built by US Army engineers around eight grass runways, with 180 revetments in the complex. It was known to the U.S. Army as APO 713 Unit 1 (bombers) and Unit 2 (fighters). The field was used by American fighters, light bombers, and liaison aircraft as a forward airfield during late 1943 through the middle of 1944. During 1944 and 1945, the airfield was used by the Royal Australian Air Force (RAAF).

After fierce fighting in the Battle of Kaiapit, the area that became the airfield was taken, and the first P-40 Kittyhawk fighter squadron began operating from Gusap in November of 1943. An all-weather fighter runway was completed in January 1944. The airstrip at Gusap "paid for itself many times over in the quantity of Japanese aircraft, equipment and personnel destroyed by Allied attack missions projected from it." (Hugh J. Casey, *Airfield and Base Development.*)

A silk map was given to all the pilots when they left for their missions. It was their escape map with the latest intelligence on local terrain and enemy positions. The reason for the choice of silk for the map was due to its water-resistance. It was going to be needed after either a dunking in the ocean or a drenching in the rain forest, so the map needed to be as waterproof as possible. Ralph still has one in his possession.

The Battle of Hollandia (code-named Operation Reckless) was an engagement between American and Japanese forces that took place in the spring of 1944. Hollandia was a port on Humboldt Bay on the north coast of New Guinea, a part of the Dutch East Indies, and was the only anchorage between Wewak to the east, and Geelvink Bay to the west. It had been occupied by the invading Japanese during the invasion of the Dutch East Indies in 1942 and had become a base for their expansion to the east towards Papua New Guinea.

In the spring of 1944 the Allied South West Pacific Command determined that the area should be seized and developed into a staging post for their advance along the north coast of New Guinea and to the Philippines. This would be about the time that Ralph got his impression of General MacArthur's personality: "He wasn't interested in the Army Air Corps until he got to New Guinea, then it was 'his' Air Force."

Initial operations commenced in the second week of March 1944 with air raids in which the U.S. 5th Air Force and the RAAF attacked Japanese airfields along the New Guinea coast from Wewak to the Vogelkop and on Biak Island. On 30 March and continuing to 3 April these air forces attacked Hollandia itself and the airfields on the Sentani plain. Fortunately achieving complete surprise, they were able to destroy nearly 100 aircraft on the ground.

Hollandia Airfield after 5th Air Force raids

Easterling flew in a P-40 on "Black Sunday," 16 April 1944, trying to reach Hollandia. A terrible front moved in and flying was treacherous. Thirty-seven aircraft were lost that day, and fifty-four flight crew perished. Ralph felt fortunate that he had been assigned to patrol down at the "home end" and so made it safely back to base.

Operation Reckless was an unqualified success, and the loss of Hollandia made the Japanese strategic defense line to the west and to the east untenable. The landings at Hollandia were followed just four weeks later by landings at Wakde, Sarmi and Toem, to the west. (S. Woodburn Kirby, *The War against Japan*.)

Easterling did have an engine die on him while flying a P-40 one day. Fortunately, it was only a test hop, as the magneto in the plane had failed the previous day. About fifteen miles from base, flying at 8,000 feet, his engine just quit for no apparent reason. He radioed in, "Please clear strip!" Coming in "dead sticking," as he neared the air strip, a tanker came across the runway, directly in his path. Ralph cleared the tanker with his landing wheels flying just barely over it. Afterwards, he "got the sergeant by the collar and asked if he was asleep."

Lockheed P-38 Lightning

To accompany MacArthur to the Philippines, Ralph transferred over to the P-38 while stationed on Biak Island. Having had all that P-40 flying experience, the P-38 "felt like heaven." The P-38 had distinctive twin booms and a central nacelle containing the cockpit and armament, so it looked like an awkward bird, to say the least. The P-38 was used for interception; dive bombing; level bombing; ground attack; night fighting; photo reconnaissance; radar and visual pathfinding for bombers and evacuation missions; and extensively as a long-range escort fighter when equipped with drop tanks under its wings. It was the aircraft of America's top aces: Richard Bong (40 victories), Thomas McGuire (38 victories) and Charles H. MacDonald (27 victories).

MacArthur giving award to Richard Bong

The P-38 was unusually quiet for a fighter, the exhaust muffled by the turbo-superchargers. It was extremely forgiving and could be mishandled in many ways but the rate of roll in the early versions was too slow for it to excel as a dogfighter. (Bill Gunston, *Aircraft of World War II.*)

While the P-38 reached the "zenith" of its use in the Pacific, the cockpit often got very hot for the pilots. Opening a window while in flight caused buffeting by setting up turbulence through the tailplane, so there was no good solution for the heat. Pilots on low altitude assignments would often fly their plane while stripped down to the bare minimum of clothing and necessities: shorts, tennis shoes, and a parachute. Minus the parachute, this was also relaxation wear.

Easterling in the cockpit of a P-40 (RE)
(Dress code was rather relaxed on the islands!)

Easterling and other pilots taking a break (RE)

P-38 cockpit

A subtle smile (RE)

While the P-38 could not out-turn the Zero and most other Japanese fighters when flying below 200 mph, its superior speed coupled with a good rate of climb meant that it could "utilize energy tactics, making multiple high-speed passes at its target." Als, its focused firepower was deadly to the lightly-armored Jap warplanes. "The concentrated, parallel stream of bullets allowed aerial victory at much longer distances than fighters carrying wing guns." (David Donald, *The Encyclopedia of World Aircraft*.)

The "Yippee"

General George C. Kenney, commander of the 5th Air Force operating in New Guinea, wrote that he could not get enough P-38s. He sent repeated requests for more. In the Pacific theater overall, the P-38 downed over 1,800 Japanese aircraft, with more than 100 pilots becoming aces by downing five or more enemy aircraft. Over 10,000 Lightnings were made, and the 5,000th Lightning built, a P-38J-20-LO, was painted bright vermilion red, and had the name YIPPEE painted on the underside of the wings in big white letters as well as the signatures of hundreds of factory workers. In-flight footage of the YIPPEE P-38 can be seen in the pilot episode of the 1960s "Green Acres" television series.

One day, Easterling was flying a P-38 out of the Tacloban air strip on Leyte, in the Philippines. He was approaching take-off speed, when he hit a drainage ditch filled with rocks and blew a tire. Unable to keep the plane under control, he spun and crashed into three other P-38s, which were all lined up on the edges of the air strip, and so tore up four P-38s in all. Amazingly, all were later repaired.

On another day, with the temperature soaring to 100 degrees, Ralph found himself aiming at a target down in the jungle. He dropped his tanks in case they could hit a dead limb and explode. He tried to pull up another twenty feet, and clipped his right wing on a tree. Fortunately, it did not depreciate his control of the aircraft and he returned safely to base. This was the only "combat damage" he suffered during the war.

One of the more interesting sights Ralph saw was on an escort mission, in May of 1944, escorting B-24 Liberators from Hollandia to Biak Island. The planes were flying at about 12,000 feet. Suddenly, flashes of light came from above. The light fingered its way down around the planes, making the sky glow. The Japs were releasing phosphorus bombs – anything the debris touched would burn right through. Fortunate as always, Easterling and his plane came through intact.

During his last six months overseas, Easterling was the head of a training squadron of pilots of P-38s and P-51s. The nimble P-51s, who flew "like you were wearing a glove," also accompanied B-29 Superfortresses on missions over Japan, taking off from Iwo Jima, where my father was stationed. Ralph added that, "of course, all fighters responded well when you got out of the P-40."

One day, Ralph received orders to choose one of his pilots to drop poison gas on men training for the invasion of mainland Japan. He didn't feel he could ask one of the other pilots to do the assignment, so he did it himself. He was told to choose his own time, and he decided to spray the gas early in the day, while the men were at breakfast. As soon as he got back from deploying the weak mix of gas, he got the report that the assignment had been successful and the men had pulled their newly issued capes over their heads and then put on their gas masks and were suffering no ill effects from the gas. However, four newsmen had *not* been issued capes or gas masks and were sick.

Easterling's longest mission was to cover a bombing run from the upper end of the Philippines, heading for the Chinese coast. He flew a P-38 for six and a half hours and then made his rendezvous with a submarine. He circled the sub, waiting for a B-17 and a PBY to show up. Both planes called in, saying they were lost, and Ralph gave them coordinates. He found this story amusing because he had to do his own navigating, flying, etc., and these larger planes had full crews, with navigators – and *they* were the ones who were lost.

Colonel Charles Lindbergh in the Southwest Pacific, shown here with Tom Maguire (RE)

Lightning Fighter Group, Tacloban Airfield, Nov 1944 (RE)

Pilots of Lightning Fighter Group (49th FG) -
Leyte- (HE 8F) - Pilots, current and former member of the Leading Fighter
Group in the world - - 537 enemy planes shot down to their credit -
- positioned in front of one of their P-38 fighters with which they
downed 37 Nips in their first week in the Philippines. They are (left
to right):

(*Total Victories)

1. George A. Walker; Commander 49th FG
2. Robert Morrisey; V AFFC
3. Gerald R. Johnson; 9th Sqd., 49th FG   22
4. Wilden E. Mathree; 7th Sqd., 49th FG   5
5. Wallace R. Jordan; 9th Sqd., 49th FG   6
6. Richard I. (Dick) Bong; 9th Sqd., 49th FG   40
7. Thomas B. (Tommy) McGuire, Jr.,; 431st Sqd., 475 FG   38
8. Robert M (Bob) DeHaven; 7th Sqd., 49th FG   14

*Total Victories added

These pictures are in front of my "new" P-38 (#42) at Tacloban, Leyte,

Philippines   Nov. 2, 1944

I, along with most of the 8th Sqd., was up on my 2nd sortie of the day

in another P-38 while #42 was being reserviced for another mission,and

while these pictures were taken.

Ralph (Pinky) Easterling

**Jerry Colona in a Bob Hope USO show, February 1945
(RE)**

**Publicity photo showing some of the planes Easterling flew –
he is flying the P-38 in the foreground (RE)**

Another shot of Easterling in the cockpit (RE)

Ralph flew numerous other planes, including the C-47, the major transport plane in the war. Somewhat anticlimactically, Easterling rotated out of the Pacific and was sent back to the United States before the war was over. He had been overseas longer than a pilot was supposed to stay – sixteen months instead of twelve – but it still must have been difficult to leave without the job being quite finished. On the ship sailing back home, he had his 21st birthday – 4 June 1945. Imagine all he had seen and experienced before he was even age twenty-one! He was back in the U.S. when the atomic bombs went off over Japan, signaling the coming end of the war. He later left the Air Corps as a First Lieutenant.

Easterling was active in forming the Air National Guard station in Charlotte. This unit was formed on 15 March 1948 with the establishment of the 156th Fighter Squadron, and is oldest unit of the North Carolina Air National Guard. It was federally recognized and activated at Morris Field, near Charlotte, and was equipped with F-47D Thunderbolts. Its mission was the air defense of the state. In 1950 the 156th was re-equipped with former World War II F-51 Mustangs and became part of Tactical Air Command (TAC) as a Tactical Reconnaissance Squadron.

Easterling in the NC Air National Guard (RE)

[162]

Easterling at

Biggs Air Force Base,

El Paso, Texas,

1952 (RE)

Front gate, Biggs Air Force Base, late 1950s

The 156th Fighter Squadron was federalized due to the Korean War on 10 October 1950. During its federalization period, the 157th was deployed to Toul-Rosières Air Base, departing for Europe in January 1952. On 9 July 1952 the activated North Carolina Air National Guard was released from active duty and returned to state control.

Easterling, however was not sent overseas, but was sent to Biggs Air Force Base, the military airport located at Fort Bliss in El Paso, Texas, which was a Strategic Air Command installation between 1947 and 1966. The 97th Bombardment Wing was the host organization at Biggs, and it operated B-29s and participated in numerous exercises, operational readiness inspections, and overseas deployments to the United Kingdom. Beginning in 1950, the 97th Bomb Wing received its first B-50 Superfortress, an improved version of the B-29 capable of delivering atomic weapons. The group element was left unmanned from 10 February 1951 to 16 June 1952, after its second forward deployment to England.

At Biggs, likely because Easterling had been in charge of training pilots in his last six months overseas in the Pacific, Ralph was assigned as a trainer. He depreciated his efforts thusly: "I towed targets for the ground pounders to shoot at." He flew the P-51 and actually went down over North Carolina, something he had never had to do while overseas. It was 1951, and Ralph was over the town of Winston-Salem on a sunny Sunday afternoon, while people were out enjoying the day. Ralph parachuted out of his plane and waved to the people to "Follow me!" instead of following the plane, as they seemed to be doing. He had to slit a hole in the chute with his knife in order to make it fall faster so he could avoid hitting a group of trees. He demonstrated he "landed *this* close" to the trees.

Easterling also got a chance to fly the North American B-45 Tornado – the United States Air Force's first operational jet bomber. "It was the only jet I flew," Ralph remarked. That, at least, must have been a highlight of his Korean experience. Ralph retired from National Guard Duty after twenty-nine years of service.

North American B-45

The 49th Fighter Group earned the Distinguished Unit Citation with three Oak Leaf Clusters for "heroism in action against an armed enemy, displaying such gallantry, determination, and esprit de corps in accomplishing its mission under extremely difficult and hazardous conditions as to set it apart and above other units participating in the same campaign." The Group also earned two Philippines Republic Presidential Unit Citations for "service in the liberation of the Philippines from 17 October 1944 to 4 July 1945."

Ralph personally received other medals: the Asiatic-Pacific Campaign Medal, the American Campaign Medal, the Victory Medal, and the Air Medal (for Heroic actions or meritorious service while participating in aerial flight). Ralph earned a National Defense Service Medal for his service with the National Guard in the Korean War, and an Armed Forces Reserve Medal for more than "ten years of honorable service in a reserve component of the United States Armed Forces Reserve." He represented the 49th Fighter Squadron in its induction into the American Airman Hall of Fame in 2010. Ralph deserves a grateful nation's thanks for his service.

Lt. Col. Ralph Easterling, USAF, retired (RE)

Easterling inducted into the American Airman Hall of Fame,
2010 (RE)

A smiling Ralph Easterling, July 2017

Sergeant Jesse E. Oxendine

Jesse Oxendine (JO)
82nd Airborne, 325th Glider Regiment

I sat on Jesse Oxendine's glassed-in porch, nestled in the treetops of his backyard, wondering how on earth he filled the birdfeeder outside when none of the glass opened as a window. Finally I asked, and an ingenious pulley system was explained to me. I would have liked to have spent many more hours on that porch.

I was to receive the privilege of learning all about Jesse's childhood and war years in what turned out to be the last year of his life. This makes the memories bittersweet. I have been told that I made a difference in his life – helped him find renewed purpose – by the book I would present to him, whipping it out from behind my back as a joyous surprise. That is one of the nicest statements I think I will ever hear, and one I deeply treasure.

Jesse Oxendine became a good friend and a frequent visitor to my home. The reason he visited so much was that he brought more and then more pictures to be included in his book; pictures I would scan and dutifully include in his memoirs, smiling all the while at his eagerness to tell not only his story, but also the story of the little town where he grew up, which has gotten somewhat of a bad rap over the years. I edited Jesse's memoirs, which started out as three essays he had written for his children. I was able to present to him a finished book, with his name on it as the author – something he never in his life ever expected to happen – especially as he turned ninety years old. What a joy this was for both of us.

During the war, Jesse was a liberator of a Nazi concentration camp – Wöbbelin camp located between Hamburg and Berlin – and spent many hours later in his life speaking to high schoolers with a Jewish friend about his (and the friend's) difficult experience. He could certainly sympathize with a minority that was horribly mistreated by its government, but he was only factual about it, never bitter. He could have had reason to be bitter: he was not even allowed to attend his state college because of racial discrimination.

Jesse was a Native American – a Lumbee Indian from Pembroke, North Carolina. His growing-up years in the 1930s reflect the good times shared by close friends and family and fond memories of his years in the Boy Scouts. The leader of his troop was a kind man who really cared about the boys and left a lasting impression on Jesse.

Jesse (left) as an Eagle Scout (JO)

I was born in 1926 and things were a little rough back then, but we always had plenty to eat. We lived in town, but we always had two hogs, a cow, and chickens. On top of that, we always had a garden. My mother did a lot of canning during the summer. I think back then, just about everybody went to church. There was one black church, one white church, and several Indian churches. Not that the Indians were better, there were just more of them.

[171]

Jesse (middle) circa 1930 (JO)

Jesse remembered things like dinners on the church grounds, his first love letter in the fourth grade, and the county fair. He also remembered playing games with his friends such as marbles – "rolling to the line" being the favorite game – simple games like hopscotch, and pastimes like collecting Superman comics. One of the more important games was "Cowboys and Indians." Being Native American gave this childhood game a different twist for Jesse:

> "Cowboys and Indians" was one of our favorites, but nobody wanted to be the Indian, in the movies they were the bad guys and they always lost. That turned us against being what we already were, Indian. Does that

make sense? As a young boy, going to the movies on Saturdays was the bright spot of the week, and the movie was always an anti-Indian and pro-cowboys shoot out. Inside the theatre I didn't want to be an Indian, but when I came out I was OK. Why were Indians different in the movies? Outside the movie house they were OK, but inside the movie house, the only good Indian you ever saw was "Tonto," the Lone Ranger's sidekick. How did this feel to a little nine or ten year old Indian boy! As a young boy I knew there were good Indians, our town and community were made up of them. Why did they have to be so bad in the movies! This story was being told in theatres on Saturdays all over the country. It had its effect: the word "Indian" meant "danger." I wanted to be the cowboy – I did not want to be white – just a cowboy. The cowboy would smile and be happy; the Indian never smiled and was never happy. I wanted to be the cowboy. The cowboy had a family; the Indian didn't have a family. I wanted to be the cowboy. The cowboy could sing and had a beautiful voice, the Indian could only holler and jump up and down. I wanted to be a cowboy. The cowboy had a beautiful horse and saddle, in other words, he had it all. Were the cowboys the only happy people?

Years later when I was married and had children, I took them up to Boone to visit "Tweetsie." (Tweetsie Railroad is a family oriented railroad and Wild West theme park located between Boone and Blowing Rock, North Carolina.) We went for a train ride and would you believe, the Indian story started again! The train was stopped by a group of wild Indians (white kids from the local college playing as Indians) my kids (Indians) were frightened to death by what was going on. A cowboy

(Fred Kirby) came to the rescue and ran all those bad Indians away and saved the day for us. Fred Kirby, the cowboy, was now my kid's hero; he got rid of those bad Indians that were going to rob us all.

Jesse worked at his father's service station on Saturdays, always hoping for a little pay at the end of the day. He was paid in change, never paper money. Later, when his father began operating the local movie theater, Jesse ran the projector.

Even before the war started for the U.S., Jesse's oldest brother signed up for the Army Air Corps. Jesse collected scrap iron and sold it to a local man paying ten cents per one hundred pounds. The iron was going to support the war effort.

Right before the war started in Europe the government started building Army camps all around and jobs were everywhere. Pickup trucks were seen leaving town every morning taking a load of men to work at Fort Bragg, Camp McCall, or the Laurinburg-Maxton Air Base. Soldiers were beginning to come into town to see how the girl situation was and maybe see a movie. You could hear the artillery guns firing all the way from Fort Bragg. Things were changing in our little town. Troop trains were passing through going north and south. Trains loaded with all kinds of military equipment were a daily thing going by on the Atlantic Coast Line Railroad.

Jesse remembered where he was when he heard about the attack on Pearl Harbor:

One Sunday some of my friends and I were playing in the field next to the house – it was December 7, 1941, when Mama and Papa drove up and told us the

Japanese had bombed Pearl Harbor. I had never heard of the place and had no idea where it was, but I knew what that meant.

Jesse and some of his high school classmates, 1944 (JO)

By 1944, his oldest brother was flying bombing missions over Germany from England, his next oldest brother was in Europe, and the next brother was in the Pacific. Pembroke residents lived through air raid drills and blackouts, however, "People were fairly happy, most everybody had a job, but when word came that one of our boys had been killed, that changed everything, and our attention went back to what was going on overseas."

When Jesse graduated from high school, his oldest brother was already back in the U.S., having completed the required combat missions safely. He remembered listening to the D-Day reports on the radio. "It was not long before the telegrams began coming in telling of the local boys that had been wounded or killed." Jesse had to live with the effects of the war long before he had to participate in it, unlike those men who signed up in the first throes of excitement at the war's beginning. "Sometime later I had caught Uncle Sam's eye and he sent me greetings from the military. I had just turned eighteen and that's all it took. I remember my dad was just sick when he came home that day with that letter. He and Mama already had three boys in the service and they thought that was enough and now they wanted me...I always told my brothers, the war didn't end until I went in and took care of things."

Oxendine took the oath at Camp Croft, South Carolina and was issued a uniform at Fort Bragg, North Carolina. He mentioned something that perhaps few might think about: "A troop train was waiting for us to take us to WHO KNOWS WHERE. I didn't like that at all. We pulled out about 12:30 am and headed south...I woke up at daylight and we were in South Carolina. It occurred to me that Mama and Papa didn't know where I was and I had just turned eighteen. They had always known where I was." Jesse wound up in Camp Robinson, Arkansas, where he completed his training in only thirteen weeks, due to the Battle of the Bulge speeding things up. More men were needed at the front.

Next, Oxendine was sent to Fort Meade, Maryland, and then overseas, sailing from Boston on the USS *Wakefield* on March 1st 1945 and arriving in Liverpool, England on March 8th. Soon, he was on an old French freighter crossing the English Channel.

We pulled into Le Havre, France, the next morning and in doing so, our ship got hung up on a sunken ship or something and they had to send out landing craft to get us onto the dock. We had to climb down on ropes to get into the landing craft. I had seen that so many times in the movies.

Jesse was assigned to the 82nd Airborne Division, the 325th Glider Regiment. His home base was in Sissonne, France a few miles north of Reimes. In mid-March, he was moved up to the front which was at that time in Cologne, Germany. "I could tell the difference between our gunfire and the Germans. The German machine gun fired much faster than ours." Oxendine was serving as a platoon runner. He would take a message or order from the company commander down to the platoon on the river. "I was always afraid of being 'jumped' or shot on the way down there, because we knew there were Germans still hiding on our side of the river."

Jesse was assigned to accompany the British 2nd Army, with whom he moved up to Northern Germany and crossed the Elbe one evening, planning to take the town of Ludwigslust the next day. Now Jesse would see the unbelievable: man's inhumanity not only to man, but also to innocent women, children, and seniors.

After crossing the river we went into the woods and dug fox holes where we spent the night. We got up at day break the next morning and were given a supply of ammo. Each man was given two bandoleers of bullets and two hand grenades. The Russians were east of us, not far away. We had the Germans on the run. We met little resistance as we moved towards our objective. We then came across this camp. What we saw was something we had never seen anything like; we were just stunned. This was not war, what was it? Who were all these people? Dead bodies lying all over the place, men with no flesh on their bodies; they were beginning to look alike. You could see the outline of their skulls making them look alike. We began asking questions, but there was no one to answer. Then we heard the word, Jews! What was with the Jews! To me, the Jews were like everybody else. Were they disliked by some that dislike the Indians and other minorities? In the movies the Indians were always the bad guys and we know how a lot of people felt about the black man. Had the Jews joined this lot? I can say now, I never did feel that dislike for the Indian while I was in the Service. I think the movies created a lot of that feeling. As far as this camp, I didn't realize what part of history I had seen until the Nuremberg Trials started sometime after the war. The unbelievable pictures I could have taken if only I would have had a camera. What the German people did to the Jewish people, I feel, will be remembered lots longer than the war itself. It was also during the Nuremberg trials that Goering reminded the American judge of the way the whites had treated the Native American Indians.

Pair remember Holocaust

BY STEVE HUFFMAN
Salisbury Post

LANDIS — In May 1945, as an 18-year-old Army private, Jesse Oxendine helped liberate a Nazi concentration camp.

A day or so following the liberation, one of his division's cooks accidentally cracked an egg and, without a second thought, tossed it out a window as trash.

Soon thereafter, Oxendine saw a recently freed concentration camp survivor, who happened to be walking by the Army camp, looking at the cracked egg lying in the dirt.

The man — starved for years — stooped, carefully raked the egg into his hand and then swallowed it.

Oxendine said the scene has remained with him a lifetime, and Tuesday morning he shared it with students at South Rowan High School.

"It was a raw egg," Oxendine told about 160 sophomores and juniors gathered in the Media Center. "He ate it and the shell. Part of it was dirt."

REMEMBERING: Henry Hirschmann (right) talks with former 82nd Airborne soldier Jesse Oxendine, who helped liberate concentration camps during WWII.

Oxendine, a 78-year-old Charlotte resident and retired pharmacist, addressed the students as part of their studies of history, specifically their studies of World War II. Most of the students are enrolled in either honors English or history classes.

Accompanying Oxendine Tuesday was Henry Hirschmann, who survived the horrors of a Nazi death camp.

Now 84, Hirschmann travels with Oxendine to schools and other gatherings, sharing the stories of a liberator and a survivor.

Their opportunities to do so, they realize, are running short. As Hirschmann put it, "We are in the winter of our lives."

Oxendine, a Lumbee Indian, was drafted into the Army as World War II wound to a close. On Tuesday, he asked if anyone in attendance was 18, the age he was when he played a role in the liberation of Nazi Germany's Wobbelin concentration camp.

A couple of South Rowan students said they are 18, and Oxendine told them: "No 18-year-old boy should ever have to experience what I did."

But Oxendine said that in a way his experiences shaped him for a lifetime. He referred to the human skeletons he and other GI's helped free, of bodies "stacked like cordwood."

The carnage the U.S. soldiers witnessed at Wobbelin, Oxendine said, was the worst of man's inhumanity to man.

"I didn't think one human being could treat another human being like that," Oxendine said.

SAD STORY: Junior Heather Huffman listens as Henry Hirschmann talks about his trials.

Jim Pope, a history teacher at South Rowan, said events like Tuesday's help students put a face to events they would otherwise have only read about in a textbook.

"You can talk about it in books all day, but it's just not the same," Pope said. "Nothing beats the primary resource."

Michael Landers, an English teacher who played an important role in bringing Oxendine and Hirschmann to South Rowan, said the students were enthralled.

"They're very attentive," Landers said. "They've never heard anything like this before."

Oxendine, a native of Pembroke, was a member of the 82nd Airborne Division's glider regiment. His division was responsible for the capture

See HOLOCAUST, page 3C

Later in life, Oxendine would devote time and energy to making sure young people knew what happened in the Holocaust so that it will never happen again. (JO)

Oxendine posing with bayoneted rifle (JO)

Oxendine had the unexpected thrill of witnessing a mass German surrender. The 21st German Army Group, with 150,000 troops, gave up to the 82nd, which had only had 11,000 men there at the time. He and some of the boys looked all around for a Luger pistol, without any of the Germans trying to escape – they were that desperate not to surrender to the Russians.

Next, Jesse took glider training at the nearby German dirt airfield. He had to make five glider rides to qualify for his glider wings. "After I had made my glider rides, I ran over and asked one of the pilots of a C-47 if I could take a ride in one of the two planes and he said 'OK.' That was my first plane ride. I flew in a glider before I flew in a plane."

Soon after this, Oxendine's unit moved back to its base in France by train, going through Hamburg, and later to Epinal, France to get new uniforms. There they were told that they had been selected to occupy Berlin with the English, French, and Russians. Jesse turned nineteen years of age in Epinal, July 20th 1945.

Oxendine (4th from left) in Berlin (JO)

Oxendine's first impression of Berlin:

Shortly after this we went to Berlin by way of Frankfurt and Potsdam. Most of the time we traveled on

[181]

"40 & 8s" – these were regular box cars. They would carry forty men or eight horses; no seats, just straw to lie on. We were glad to get there. Our bombers and the Russians had done a good job on the city. It was what you would call a "has been." Ha. Hitler had planned to make it the most beautiful city in the world, now look at it.

What was it like to be one of the occupying Army? Jesse's description turns where a young man's heart usually does:

The Americans treated the Germans better than the Russians did. We were not supposed to fraternize with the local German ladies but you know how G.I.'s are, they wanted to be friendly, they had fought long enough. It wasn't too long before most of the men had a friend. I don't guess I was any different from most of the other boys, and like I say, the girls were real friendly. My buddy, Frenchie, and I met two sisters, Anna Marie and Hilda.

I first met Anna Marie at this club over on Herman Platz one night when I was there with some of my buddies. We were sitting at a table, just talking and listening to the music. They were having a beer, I was having a coke. I turned and noticed these two girls were sitting at a table nearby with two real young boys. The boys looked to be about fifteen years of age. So, since these boys were so young I knew they were not boyfriends. The younger girl was beautiful. To my surprise, I got up and went over to their table and asked if I might join them, and to my surprise again, they said yes. I must say, I was surprised at me being so bold doing this. I guess I had picked this up from watching men do it in the movies, but still this was not my mode of action. Ha. With my little bit of German and their little bit of English, we started a little bit of conversation. After a short time, Anna Marie held her hand over next to mine and I could tell she was trying to ask me my nationality. I told her I was American Indian; she smiled and seemed to be excited. I'm sure she had studied about the American Indians in school. She was by far the best looking girl I had seen since arriving in Berlin. We hit it off real well after talking for some time and I knew the next thing to do was to get her sister a boyfriend. I'm sure they had come there hoping to meet someone and I was glad that someone was me.

Anna Marie was my age and Hilda had been married, but her husband, who was a pilot in the German Air Force, had been killed in Italy. We did not talk too much about the war and what we heard or saw. Looking back, I wish I had asked her more about what it was like growing up in Germany. Did she see Hitler? Did she join some of Hitler's Youth Clubs for girls? After all, she and I were enemies of each other at one time and now that is hard to believe. What was it like when the Russians were taking the city, where were they hiding? What about food, did she have any brothers in service? As much as we talked, how did we leave all these questions out of our conversations? I guess my total thoughts were, "the war is over." She did tell me about how bad the raids were, but that's about all.

The Army had a club where we could take our dates or we could go to a movie. Our mess halls served good food and plenty of it. The locals did not have very much to eat. The club we had did not serve any food or drinks; the only thing they provided was a very good orchestra for dancing. We dated the whole time I was in Berlin and would see each other several times a week over around Herman Platz. They lived in the Russian sector of Berlin and Herman Platz was in the American sector. At that time there was no wall and you could travel around the city with no problem. I told her about my girlfriend back home and we had a good understanding about that. We knew why I was there and it would be for only a short time. This was a wartime romance and these had been going on all through history. She was a very nice young lady and I'm sure later she made some young man a very nice wife. We were the age of people that had to take part in this time of history. I returned home and was glad to start my life over, but she and I didn't forget the short time we saw each other in that far away city right after that awful war. We exchanged letters about how things were going for several years after the war. I pray her life has been as blessed as mine has.

Jesse had put in for Staff Sergeant but all promotions had been frozen due to the fact that the 101th Airborne was being deactivated and they were sending all the "low point" men to the 82nd. That meant a lot of Sergeants from their outfit would be joining the 82nd, and more Staff Sergeants would not be needed. That knocked Jesse out of his promotion. All his brothers had made Staff Sergeant, so this was a great disappointment. Sergeants in the U.S. Army command squads of as many as ten enlisted men, and Staff Sergeants command squads of the same size, so the main difference is in the rate of pay. However, a Staff Sergeant could be placed in command of sergeants and could earn promotion to higher ranks. Jesse did earn a Bronze

[184]

Star medal, and I have seen a certificate stating such, but he never really described which event caused him to earn it.

Oxendine told more of his experiences while occupying Berlin:

Berlin was where everybody wanted to wind up. How lucky were we boys. Of course, the Army wanted their best outfit up there. We were there from July till December and it was the place to be. We were there when we heard about the bomb being dropped on Japan. The people back home didn't know it, but we were having trouble with the Russians then. One night an American soldier would get killed and the next night, a Russian soldier would get killed. We were killing each other. I had a little "run-in" with some Russians soldiers one night. My buddy Frenchie and I had walked the two girls home, they lived in the Russian sector, and on the way back we got lost. I think there were four of these Russian soldiers. They wanted to buy a pistol. Somehow we managed to tell them we didn't have one, but would come back the next night and sell them one. All four were drinking. The nice thing about it, I had a pistol but they didn't know it. Boy, was I afraid! If they started anything, I was going to shoot all four of them in the stomach and take off running, hoping I would not kill them, but making them unable to catch us. My pistol was that small 22 caliber, and they being drunk, I thought we could get away without killing one of them. Thank goodness, we were able to walk away without any trouble, but we were still lost. About that time, we met up with another G.I. that had taken his girlfriend home and he knew how to get back to Tempelhof Airport. We knew how to get to our apartment; it was only a few blocks from there. That was my last visit to the Russian sector. Like I said, there was no wall back then.

The first time we went for a tour of Berlin we went out to see where the 1936 Olympics were held. Oh, what a beautiful stadium this was. I could not tell if there was any damage to it at all. I walked through some of the offices to see if I might find something of interest and to my surprise, I found three 1936 Olympic pins. Boy, was that luck! There were several anti-aircraft guns placed out in this area. I am sure these very guns had shot at my oldest brother's plane when he was on a raid of the city.

We had football games while we were up there. Most of the Army outfits formed football teams. I went to one game we were having and saw this boy that was playing on the other team and I was almost sure I recognized him. After the game was over, I went down on the field to see him, and it turned out to be a boy from home. We also had Company parties once in a while. I don't think we were supposed to invite our German girls, but they were there. Our big night club was over at Herman Platz, and we hung out there. The streetcars were running, so we could get around on them. So many boys would be hanging onto the streetcar, you couldn't even see it. All the bridges in Berlin had been blown up so you could only ride a streetcar between each canal, get off, walk across a wooden bridge, catch another streetcar, and ride it to the next blown out bridge until you got to your destination. It took about three or four streetcars to get from our apartment to Herman Platz. We ate real good while we were there. I don't remember why, but I never did have to pull K.P. In fact, I think I only pulled it one time the whole time I was in the Army. I just don't know why, but I'm glad.

Back to the food: We had plenty to eat. We boys always took out more than we could eat, because we knew the German kids would be standing outside with their little buckets wanting us to put our leftovers into their buckets. The officers never did get on us about doing that. Once in a while, we would take a sandwich with us on a date knowing the girls didn't have much to eat. There was no place where you could go buy food. Whenever we went to our club you had to take what you were going to drink. I would go with the boys to get beer but I never did drink it.

Several of the "high point" men were being sent home by now. Word came out in the "Stars and Stripes" that the 82nd Airborne was going home as a unit and would be stationed at Fort Bragg, North Carolina or Camp Hood, Texas. On top of that, we were to parade down Fifth Avenue in New York City to celebrate the end of World War II. Can you just imagine how I felt?? Home at last. I wanted to send Mama, and my sisters a little something from Berlin so I went into what used to be a store and got Mama a bust of "Nefertiti" and got my sisters a little ornament of "Mary and Jesus." I had to pay for them with cigarettes. The money was no good. I was glad when I heard from home and knew these things had got home safe.

Jesse next gave his account of coming back to the United States after the war:

We left Berlin about the middle of December. We were on "18 wheelers" with no top. We went back to the American sector of Germany and got on a train. We then went, I think, to Camp Chesterfield to wait for a ship to

[187]

take us to England. We stayed there for a while then went to Le Havre to take a ship over to Southampton. From Southampton we went to Tidworth, a British Army camp on the coast. While there I got a pass to London on Christmas Day 1945. I went by train to London and stayed at a USO club. I remember the bed had sheets on it. We could even take our clothes off at night when going to bed. Ha. They sure did feel good. That was the first time I had slept on sheets since going overseas. While eating breakfast the next morning, I noticed this G.I. sitting at the next table. I thought I knew him and he kept looking at me so I went over to his table and he was from Union Chapel. That's a little area just outside of Pembroke. I can't remember his name, but I saw him later when we got home.

I wanted to see London, so I got me a taxi and told the driver to show me the town. Ha. The other boys wanted to sleep. It was a fun Christmas even though I was not at home, because I knew I was on my way home and that kept me in good spirits.

December 29th came and we got on the train heading for Southampton to board our ship. What a sight that was when we pulled into the dock and saw the big, beautiful ship just waiting for us. As we went up the gang plank we were given a certificate stating that we had returned to the States aboard the *Queen Mary* and the date that we had boarded. I still have mine. We were given a card showing where we would be sleeping. I still have that. My room was B-15. Normally, it was a room for two, but I think there were eight of us.

The hammocks were about the same as those on the USS *Wakefield* [the ship on which he sailed while going overseas]. We pulled out late that afternoon,

December 29th 1945, a day I will never forget. I thought of all the boys that would not be coming back. There were a lot of them that had gone over on the *Queen Mary*, I'm sure. We spent a lot of time just walking around looking the ship over; they let us do that. Later, I looked up the record of this trip. There were 11,346 troops on board and we traveled 3,136 miles coming back. It took us five days, one hour and thirty-four minutes to make the trip back. And I loved every minute of it, coming back home. We had a calm trip going over but boy, did we run into a storm coming back. The waves were breaking over the bow and the ship was rolling like a ball. I went up to the front of the ship and the wind was blowing like everything. The ship was barely moving. I would love to have seen a smaller ship out there, just to have seen how it could have stayed afloat. The storm lasted most of one day, but then things began to calm down and we picked up speed again. I had a camera so I was able to take a few pictures on the way back aboard the ship.

I remember eating in the large dining room of the ship. They were able to feed a lot of troops at the same time aboard her. Even though there were no subs looking for us now, we still had our drills in case of trouble. We had a big party on New Year's Eve, which would have been December 31st, 1945. The 82nd band came out and played all kinds of music and I'm sure there were some drinks around, maybe beer and even cokes for some of we boys. And to think, only two more days before we would see the good old USA, and then to be home! What a feeling that was. We didn't see another ship going over or coming back, after all that's a big ocean and besides, I was now only looking for New York.

Coming home on the *Queen Mary* (JO)

We were now almost home and I do believe some of the boys played poker all the way across. There were more poker games going on there than in Las Vegas.

I felt real good when I laid down the night of January 2nd knowing the next morning I would see lights, land, and then New York City. I could hardly wait. I must have gotten up in the middle of the night to get me a good spot on the deck so I could see everything. I remember the lights, but the fog was real thick that morning, but I knew what it was, we were back and we had made it. I would like to think that I made a little prayer.

And They'll Parade on 5th Ave.

Jesse was on top over-looking the life boats...

WELCOME HOME! Returning heroes of the famous 82nd Airborne Div. jam the Queen Mary's rails, greeted by wounded GI, by Red Cross workers, friends, lin.

82nd Airborne returns home to the U.S. (JO)

[191]

Oxendine went on to describe pulling into New York harbor and participating in the huge parade of returning soldiers, as well as seeing his mother for the first time since he had left for overseas:

We were well-welcomed back home. Boats came out shooting water up into the sky and there were a lot of people on our dock. The mayor of the city came out to welcome us, camera crews and newspaper people were all over the place. We had made a small donation to help some of the war brides with babies that were on board. When we got off we had a full field pack and our duffel bag, in fact, everything we owned including our rifle. Boy, was it good to just step on American soil.

We got on a ferry and crossed the river. Trucks were waiting on us to take us out to Camp Shanks. We were to be there until we had the parade which was to take place January 12th. That was a long time to wait before we could get home. But to take part in the Victory Parade of World War II, that was quite an honor. It was an honor for our division and it was an honor for me, now looking back. There were a lot of men that took part in that war, but only a small percent that took part in this celebration of victory. So now, looking back, I think I was lucky to have been one of the men that got to march down 5th Avenue that day.

As soon as we got out to Camp Shanks we got a real good meal. The first or second night we were there we got a pass to New York City. Now that was something. I would not have gone alone, but with a group of these guys, I would have gone any place. An Army truck took us into town and put us off at Times Square. First, we found a place to make a telephone call.

You might know who we were calling, HOME. I told the operator I wanted 2481 in Pembroke, North Carolina and was calling collect. I don't remember who answered the phone, but most of my family was there. That was the first phone call I had made since I left home the previous year. What a great time in my life this was!

My family had heard of the parade that was going to take place in New York, so they, or some of them, decided to go see it. Why not, if Jesse was going to be in it! Ha. I tried to tell them where I would be in the parade, and to be on the left side of the street. After we boys made our telephone calls, we went looking for some place to go. For some reason we went to some restaurants and fancy night clubs; we were just looking. We couldn't eat because we didn't have that kind of money. The people in the fancy night clubs got a bang out of us, just walking around looking. They knew we had just gotten back from overseas. We were just a group of small town boys looking this big city over and weren't afraid of anything. I got in trouble the next night, I called my girlfriend and she had found out I had called home the night before. I didn't want to call collect so she could understand that. Now, seventy years later, I don't remember how I worked that out.

We had almost a week to wait for the parade. We probably had a "dry run" for the parade; I just can't remember what we did that week. When the big day came, we got on trucks and went into New York. It looked as though we might have a little rain so we took our rain coats. By the time we got to where the parade was to start, it cleared up and we placed our rain coats into a big pile. Boy, did we look sharp! When we fell-in, I got in the second column on the left; I was about the

10th or 12th man back. The man on the outside column had to look straight ahead, me being on the second column I could look to the left and look for my family if they were out front. There were only four million people there that day. There was no way I was going to spot my family, but I was going to try. Would you believe, I didn't? Ha. I had not seen so many people in all my life. That was more people than the population of North Carolina back then.

There were several bands in the parade that day and it made it a little difficult to stay in step but we did. The parade made all the news that day and was shown in all the movie theatres on the "News of the Day." We even made Life Magazine. After the parade we went on back to Camp Shanks, not seeing my family. After a short time one of my buddies came in and told me my brother was looking for me. Can you just imagine how I felt? I was about to see a family member, my second oldest brother. I won't ever forget the moment. I went outside and there he was. Oh, what a day. He told me the rest of the family was still in New York, waiting in Grand Central Station. No one was supposed to get into the camp that day, so when he got there, the guard stopped him. He told the guard that he had just gotten out of service and had come to see the parade and his brother was in the camp. My brother also told the guard about his mother waiting to see her son. The guard told him he had orders to not let any one pass, BUT he would be walking on down to another point and if he walked in behind him, he would not be able to see him. When the guard turned his back to my brother, he didn't see him sneak in behind him and go into the camp. I would have loved to have hugged that guard's neck.

I got a pass and we took off for New York, it was not too far away. We got to the station, and there was my mother and family. I get tears in my eyes when I think of that even today. (I went to New York a few years ago and I went to the station just to see the spot where I met my mother). I decided to go back down to Philadelphia with them before going back to camp. I stayed late into the night and then got the train back to New York and a bus out to camp.

After returning to Fort Bragg, Jesse received a thirty-day furlough and took a bus to his home town:

It was snowing like mad. The last bus going through Pembroke had just got there and the driver said it was full and could not take any more passengers. I told him I was going if I had to ride on top. He said I would have to stand up, there were no more seats. Anyway, I got on that bus. Standing up on a bus for twelve miles was nothing compared to what I had been through. Buses back then were always full, everybody didn't have a car. Boy, was I glad to see Pembroke when the bus rolled in. Most everything was closed but this one station. It was a gas station and a little eating joint. There were several young people in there. I walked in and the owner saw me and came running. He was a friend of my family. He gave me a big hug and then went to his telephone. He picked up the phone and called my home. My mother answered, and he said, "Guess who I have down here?" Everybody was looking and was glad to see me. About that time my oldest brother walked in and saw me. No one was expecting me that night; I had wanted to surprise them. Anyway, he had Papa's car so he took me on home. When I got home several members of the family were there. I had seen Mama in New York, but I had not seen Papa and some of the other family members. What a night to remember! The war was over and the fourth son had come home. How blessed we had been.

It was so nice to be home at last. It must have been around the 15th or 16th of January 1946. So many of the boys were home now but there were a few still overseas. All three of my brothers had already been discharged from the service. I had about five more months to serve. I think it was June 29th when I got out. My girlfriend came home for a few days; she was now working in Charlotte. You can imagine how glad I was to see her. It had been a long time and now life was beginning to seem normal. It was hard to realize that most everybody was back home again; the war had been going on so long. Then we realized that some of the boys would not be returning; that was hard to believe.

I spent a lot of time just lying around the house – I remember that real well, because I was kind of surprised at that. I guess I wanted to make sure I was at home. I spent a lot of my time in Charlotte and my girl would come home on the weekends. Papa was real good about letting we boys use his car. Only a few of the boys had a car back then. Papa had bought the theatre back and now we were back in the theatre business. [Then] my furlough ended and I had to report back to Fort Bragg.

After his furlough, Oxendine "got back to Army business." He took glider rides on a regular basis, using the base at Pope Field. He also took part in several parades in some of the local towns. His division went down to Fort Benning, Georgia to put on an Airborne demonstration for members of the United Nations. "That was a big thing for us." Jesse described this important event:

The day of the exercise we took off in gliders at Fort Benning and flew to a base across the river in Alabama where a large group of people were waiting to see an airborne landing. As soon as our glider landed we were to get out and run to an assembly area. That day I was stuck with a B.A.R., which was an automatic rifle, and boy was it heavy. As we came in another glider cut in front of us and we had to cut away from it making us land a long distance from where we had planned to land. Now I had to run about twice as far. It's a good thing I was in shape, having all those members of the U.N. there watching us. Everything turned out OK and they were pleased with our exercise.

Oxendine (2nd from left) on Veterans Day, 1947 (JO)

After he was discharged at the end of June, it was time for Jesse to decide what to do with the rest of his life and the question of attending college came to the forefront:

We veterans got together and talked about where we had been and some of the things we had done and it came up about the University at Chapel Hill. We boys had been in the Service for some time and now the war was over and we wanted to go to college. We had the college there in Pembroke that was for the Indians but some of the boys wanted to go to Chapel Hill to take courses that were not offered at Pembroke – and to think that was not possible. Pembroke State College was built for Indians and that was where they wanted us to go. It was so outrageous we just sat around and laughed about it. We had fought and died with the students at Chapel Hill, but we could not study and learn with them. Other states were willing to help us, but not the Tar Heels, and to think the Germans, who we had been fighting, could come over here and attend our University. What in the world was going on! Today the young people can't believe that ever happened, but it did.

The transition from military service to civilian life can often be a difficult one. After a short time of indecision, Oxendine was directed toward becoming a pharmacist:

As for me, I didn't know what I wanted to do. Living in Pembroke you had two choices, teaching or farming. I didn't think I wanted to teach and I didn't know a thing about farming. I entered college at Pembroke State, not knowing what to do. One day my cousin came up to me at the service station and asked, "Jesse, why don't you go off and study Pharmacy and I will go off and study Medicine and we will come back here and go into business." That got me thinking. Our local Pharmacist went to work every day with a white shirt on and never got his hands dirty – now I liked that... I did not apply to the Pharmacy School in my home state of North Carolina because they did not accept Indians.)This means the first Native American registered pharmacist in North Carolina [Jesse] did not graduate from the State Pharmacy School.)

[At first] I gave up [the idea of] Pharmacy [as a career] and entered Kings Business College in Charlotte. After taking Business Administration, I got a job with the P & N Railroad in the accounting department here in Charlotte.

About two years later I tried my luck again on getting into Pharmacy school and was accepted at the Medical College of South Carolina in Charleston. After finishing my junior year I got a summer job at Bizzell Pharmacy and was offered a job when I graduated in 1955. I worked at Bizzell Pharmacy for two years or so and was offered a job with Kiser Drug with the possibility of part ownership.

During the time he was going to school, Jesse met and married his wife. Later, they lived in a duplex near King Drug, the renamed Kiser location. Three of their children were born there, and their youngest daughter was born after their move into a house. Sadness touched Jesse's life, as it does everyone's. By the time I knew him, he had lost two daughters and his wife, both to accident and to illness.

Much of Jesse's life was determined by the fact that he was Native American. Later, he would be Chairman of the Board of Trustees of the University of North Carolina at Pembroke, ensuring that Indian young people could go to a state school right there at home. Jesse remembered an amusing story of assumed discrimination that happened during the 1960s:

Jesse in front of his pharmacy (JO)

The one thing I do remember about the store on Eastway Drive [where Jesse was the pharmacist and owner] was, I was looking for help, a cashier, and several women came by and after interviewing them, I hired one. Later a gentleman came by the store from the E.E.O.C. Some lady had filed a complaint about me not hiring her because she was black. I could not believe that. She said the store was discriminating against minorities. I called my soda fountain manager over, M. R., who was black, and introduced her, I then called D. C., who was Native American, then my brother, a Native American, and me, the owner, a Native American, and then pointed to T., who was black — then I suggested that the minorities outnumbered the whites and so he might want to represent them. He shook his head and walked out. We got a big laugh about that.

Jesse Oxendine, a good friend (JO)

**Jesse appeared in Smithsonian Magazine
(Jesse turned 90 years old two months
after this photo was taken.)**

I have now met several women who have told me that they remembered Jesse from their childhoods. They took their report cards to him at the pharmacy and he gave them a free milkshake. These stories are a simple testimony to the type of person Jesse Oxendine was.

Jesse demonstrated kindness and generosity to others his whole life. I believe anyone who ever met Jesse liked him almost instantly. He made friends wherever he went. My life has been enriched for having known him, and I am honored to share part of the story that he shared with me.

Wise Words from a World War II Veteran

Now, looking back, as bad as the war was, I think the men and women that went into the Service did enrich their lives by meeting and serving with other people from all over the country and traveling all over the world seeing just how people may be so much alike and yet just how we may differ. The war made the world so much smaller. We need each other. We need to learn to talk to each other. When I was a young boy and got mad about something, I was told to count to ten before I reacted. We need to solve our problems at a table rather than on a battlefield. Think of how many lives could have been saved by only talking! I'm sure we made a lot of advances during the war that may not have come so fast during peace time, but look at the millions and millions of broken hearts it cost.

Jesse Oxendine

About the Author

Kathleen Shelby Boyett is an International Author and a Personal Historian who specializes in writing exciting and interesting family histories for her clients and assists other clients in writing their memoirs. She is a Board Member of the North Carolina Military Veterans Hall of Fame, a museum volunteer, a supporter of the Military Order of the Purple Heart, a member of the Women's National Book Association, the Mecklenburg Historical Association, and of the National Society Daughters of the American Revolution. Ms. Boyett is the author or editor of over thirty books about American History, including both nonfiction and creative nonfiction. Her books are sold at historical site and museum gift shops, as well as online.

www.shelbyboyett.webs.com

Made in the USA
Columbia, SC
14 November 2017